More Praise for *Chaotics* from Around the World

"Turbulence is erratic—and it's unpredictable. Nevertheless, we must handle it. In *Chaotics*, Kotler and Caslione don't just remind us to pay attention to early signs; they give business leaders an outstanding map for how to successfully navigate a company through crises." —*Friedrich von Metzler, Member, Partners' Committee, B. Metzler seel. Sohn & Co. Holding AG*

"Turbulence and unpredictability are the inevitable realities of the next few years. We are in truly uncharted waters, with no good maps. *Chaotics* will help your organization to navigate without one. This incredibly useful and helpful book provides clear and practical guidance to the many difficult decisions that managers and leaders need to make in turbulent times. It is like having the authors and their wisdom at your side while having to ride the white waters of the rapids ahead." —*Peter Schwartz, Monitor Global Business Network*

"[A]n operations manual to help management teams guide their companies through this global disaster. *Chaotics* is a must read for those seeking a lifeline to save their business." —*Ed Kaplan, Chairman Emeritus, Zebra Technologies*

"A very timely and practical book on how to manage and market the enterprise through prolonged turbulence. The Chaotics Management System provides an excellent blueprint for making each major business function more resilient." —*Jagdish N. Sheth, Ph.D., Charles H. Kellstadt Professor of Marketing, Goizueta Business School, Emory University, Atlanta, GA; author of* The Self-Destructive Habits of Good Companies: . . . And How to Break Them

"*Chaotics* is about real events in real time. World authorities on marketing and strategy Philip Kotler and John Caslione address the global financial crisis with experience, wisdom, and hands-on advice." —*Dr. Evert Gummesson, Professor of Marketing, Stockholm University School of Business, Sweden; author,* Total Relationship Marketing

"*Chaotics* provides rich food for thought in turbulent times. This book helps you to more deeply understand the crisis. And only if you understand will you avoid making the fatal mistakes, which are the greatest danger in a time of crisis." —*Hermann Simon, Chairman, Simon-Kucher & Partners Strategy & Marketing Consultants; author,* Hidden Champions of the 21st Century

"Today, few business leaders really understand what will change in their industries post the 2008–2009 credit crunch. Every industry will be playing by new rules. *Chaotics* is essential reading for those who want to be winners during these turbulent and uncertain times." —*Stefan Barden, Chief Executive Officer, Northern Foods plc, UK*

"In *Chaotics*, Philip Kotler and John Caslione make sense of the new turbulent world order. *Chaotics* provides a powerful and timely guide to the new realities." —*Stuart Crainer, editor of* Business Strategy Review; *creator of the Thinkers 50, UK*

"*Chaotics* provides business leaders with an invaluable framework to help them guide their enterprises wisely through the turbulence of contemporary markets. The definitive navigational map for every business leader today and for our chaotic future." —*Walter Giorgio Scott, Distinguished Professor, Università Cattolica del Sacro Cuore, Milan, Italy*

"*Chaotics* provides an extremely valuable guide to help managers transform chaos into order and take advantage of market turbulence to strengthen company leadership. This reading is a must." —*Fernando Trias de Bes, economist and writer, ESADE Business School, Barcelona, Spain; coauthor,* Lateral Marketing

"With the financial tsunami, Kotler and Caslione keenly proposed a significant new theme—*Chaotics*—to help design more management and marketing resilience in companies aiming to steer profitably through the turbulence. This book moves beyond static equilibrium economic theory to dynamic management and marketing theory." —*Professor Taihong Lu, Sun Yat-sen University; Director, China Marketing Research Center; coauthor,* Marketing Management—A China Perspective

"The appearance of *Chaotics* is extremely important at a time when many economists and financial experts are guessing—with most only giving belated explanations of the world financial crises. Kotler and Caslione have a clear view of the present economic situation, emerging trends, and even more valuable, they give practical advice on how business leaders can successfully navigate through the new turbulent economy. *Chaotics* should be the reference book for every businessman in 'The Age of Turbulence.'" —*Alexander Izhorsky, Ph.D. in economics; CEO of the Association of Marketing Research, Russia; Editor-in-Chief of the international magazine* Marketolog

"A book that should have been written ten years ago and is much in need today has finally arrived. *Chaotics* offers concrete recommendations in a systematic way, providing much needed hope in the midst of the current global economic crisis." —*Waldemar Pfoertsch, China Europe International Business School, Shanghai, China*

"*Chaotics* gives business leaders critical insights and a roadmap of systems and tools essential for today's new conditions—unpredictable turbulence. The authors' evidence is compelling, their analysis incisive, and their advice priceless for thriving in the age of turbulence." —*Linden R. Brown, Chairman, MarketCulture Strategies, Inc., Australia*

"Like turning on a bright light in a room of darkness, *Chaotics* illuminates today's formidable challenges and goes that extra step to provide a clear and practical framework for mastering the turbulence. An important and timely contribution to management and marketing." —*Randall Ringer, Managing Partner, Verse Group, LLC*

"With mastery, Kotler and Caslione describe "The New Normality of Turbulence" and elaborate on its implications for all the functions in business. The Chaotics Management System is timely and will be a lasting contribution to management." —*Eduardo Braun, Corporate Director, HSM Global*

"The metaphor of turbulence in nature is brilliant because it leads seamlessly into the need for an 'early warning system' for business. Weather forecasters have been at this a long time, and while we can't prevent the tornado, drought, or hurricane, we can prepare for it. Businesspeople must do the same . . . and the authors help you do that with tools and strategies." —*Joe Plummer, Columbia University and Olson Zaltman Associates*

Chaotics

The Business of Managing and Marketing in The Age of Turbulence

PHILIP KOTLER

AND

JOHN A. CASLIONE

AMACOM AMERICAN MANAGEMENT ASSOCIATION

NEW YORK ∎ ATLANTA ∎ BRUSSELS ∎ CHICAGO ∎ MEXICO CITY
SAN FRANCISCO ∎ SHANGHAI ∎ TOKYO ∎ TORONTO ∎ WASHINGTON, D.C.

Special discounts on bulk quantities of AMACOM books are available to corporations, professional associations, and other organizations. For details, contact Special Sales Department, AMACOM, a division of American Management Association, 1601 Broadway, New York, NY 10019.
Tel: 212-903-8316. Fax: 212-903-8083.
E-mail: specialsls@amanet.org
Website: www.amacombooks.org/go/specialsales
To view all AMACOM titles go to: www.amacombooks.org

This publication is designed to provide accurate and authoritative information in regard to the subject matter covered. It is sold with the understanding that the publisher is not engaged in rendering legal, accounting, or other professional service. If legal advice or other expert assistance is required, the services of a competent professional person should be sought.

Library of Congress Cataloging-in-Publication Data

Kotler, Philip.
Chaotics : the business of managing and marketing in the age of turbulence / Philip Kotler and John A. Caslione. — 1st ed.
    p. cm.
Includes index.
ISBN-13: 978-0-8144-1521-4
ISBN-10: 0-8144-1521-0
1. Marketing. 2. Management. 3. Business cycles. 4. Globalization. I. Caslione, John A. II. Title.
HF5415.K6244 2009
658—dc22

2009003055

Printing number
10 9 8 7 6 5 4 3 2 1

To all MBA students and to those MBA students from the Kellogg School of Management, Northwestern University, who we have trained to deal with the "rough and tumble" world of business where risk and uncertainty rules but can be handled with insight and preparedness.

Philip Kotler

To my guiding light, Donatella: my most cherished friend and dedicated partner in all that I do in my life, whom I so proudly call my lovely, beautiful, and tremendously gifted wife, for her boundless patience and unwavering commitment to me, which has inspired me to write the thoughtful chapters of this book, and to write the most inspiring and joyous chapters of my life.

John A. Caslione

C O N T E N T S

PREFACE

When the U.S. financial meltdown struck in 2008, with the seeds laid much earlier, we were asked by our clients and friends, "How deep will it be? How long will it last?" They wanted to know if it would be a short-run recession, a deep recession, or even a great depression. When asked the same question in October 2008, Gary Becker, the Nobel Prize–winning economist, said, "Nobody knows. I certainly don't know." The message: Don't trust economists who say they know.

The fact is that we are entering a new age of turbulence, and moreover, heightened turbulence. In his book *The Age of Turbulence* (Penguin Press, 2007), Alan Greenspan describes his diverse experience as the Federal Reserve chairman and one of the most powerful men in the world. Greenspan had to deal with a great number of economic disturbances and shocks for which the only recourse was to muddle through and pray. He was confronted with major issues facing the United States, such as burgeoning trade deficits and retirement funding, as well as the proper role of government regulation.

The world is more interconnected and interdependent than ever before. Globalization and technology are the two main forces that helped create a new level of *interlocking fragility* in the world economy. Globalization means that producers in one country are increasingly importing resources from other countries and increasingly exporting their output to other countries. Technology—in the form of computers, the Internet, and mobile phones—enables information to course through the world at lightning speed. News of a breakthrough discovery, a corporate scandal, or the death of a major figure is heard around the world. The good news is lower costs, but the bad news is increased vulnerability. Outsourcing has always had its defenders and its critics. While global interdependence works in everyone's favor in good times, it rapidly spreads much pain and damage in bad times.

But what is turbulence? We know it when it occurs in nature: It creates havoc in the form of hurricanes, tornados, cyclones, or tsunamis. We experience turbulence in the air from time to time when a pilot asks us to fasten our seat belts. In all these cases, stability and predictability vanish; instead, we are buffeted, bounced, and jabbed by conflicting and relentless forces. And sometimes the turbulence will be so continuous as to plunge the whole economy into a downturn, a recession, or possibly a protracted depression.

Economic turbulence creates the same impact on us as turbulence in nature. One moment we hear that Miami has built more condominiums than buyers are buying. Speculators are carrying the cost and having a hard time meeting the payments. We hear of families who have purchased their homes on NINA—"No Income, No Assets"—loans. Now they can't make their mortgage payments and are facing foreclosures. Banks start realizing that they have deadbeat assets due to securitization and hesitate to make more loans to either customers or other banks. Consumers hear this news and switch from credit-based spending to saving, causing companies that sell automobiles, furniture, and other "postponables" to suffer declining sales. These companies, in turn, announce major layoffs that result in less available consumer purchasing power. Meanwhile, companies slow down their buying from other companies, creating hardship for their suppliers, who in turn, lay off their workers.

Companies in these difficult times tend to make across-the-board cuts. They deeply reduce their new product development budgets and marketing budgets, both of which undercut their short-term recovery and long-term future. Consumers, workers, producers, bankers, investors, and other economic actors feel that they are living through an economic hurricane, a maelstrom that is unstoppable and relentless.

Hopefully, this turbulence is only short-lived. In the past, it has been. It has not been the normal state of an economy. Yes, economies often do return to "normal" conditions, but in this new era, turbulence at varying levels becomes an essential condition. A particular country may be racked by turbulence, as Iceland experienced in 2008 as its banks moved into bankruptcy. A particular industry—advertising, for example—may be racked by turbulence as companies move more of their money from thirty-second TV commercials into newer media such as websites, e-mails, blogs, and podcasts. Some markets may be turbulent, such as the housing market or the auto market. Finally, individual companies such as General Motors, Ford, and Chrysler may be buffeted by turbulence while others—Toyota or Honda, for example—may experience less of a plight.

The fact that an individual company can be living through conditions of turbulence, and if it lasts long enough, a recession, is underscored in Andy Grove's well-known book, *Only the Paranoid Survive* (Currency Doubleday, 1999). As the former CEO of Intel Corporation, Grove had to deal with all kinds of threats to Intel's preeminent position in the computer chip manufacturing business. It would take just one agile competitor to come out with a superior chip at a lower price to topple Intel. Grove had to live with uncertainty. Intel had to erect an early-warning system that would reveal signs of imminent trouble. It had to create different "what if" scenarios. And it had to preplan different responses to the different scenarios in case they occurred.

Grove had to create a system that would insure against risk and respond to uncertainty. We have a name for such a system. We call it *chaotics*. All companies must live with risk (which is measurable) and uncertainty (which is unmeasurable). They must build an early-warning system, a scenario construction system, and a quick response system to manage and market during recessions and other turbulent conditions. But our finding is that most companies operate without a chaotics system. Their defenses are scattered and insufficient. Motorola doesn't have a chaotics system. General Motors doesn't have one; nor do countless others in the United States, Europe, Asia, and in markets all around the world.

Most companies operate on the assumption of a built-in self-restoring equilibrium. Economists built price theory with equilibrium in mind. If oversupply occurs, producers will cut their prices. Sales will increase, thus absorbing the oversupply. Conversely, if a shortage occurs, producers will raise their prices to a level that will balance demand and supply. Equilibrium will prevail.

We postulate that turbulence, and especially heightened turbulence, with its consequent chaos, risk, and uncertainty, is now the normal condition of industries, markets, and companies. Turbulence is the *new normality*, punctuated by periodic and intermittent spurts of prosperity and downturn—including extended downturns amounting to recession or even depression. And turbulence has two major effects. One is vulnerability, against which companies need defensive armor. The other is opportunity, which needs to be exploited. Bad times are bad for many and good for some. Opportunity occurs when a strong company can take away a competitor's business or even acquire a weakened competitor at a bargain price. Opportunity is present when your company doesn't cut critical costs, but all your competitors do.

If we are correct, companies need a chaotics system for dealing with uncertainty. We will outline such a system and illustrate it, with cases of companies that have been victimized by chaos resulting from turbulence and many companies that exploited chaos to their advantage. We are hopeful *Chaotics* will help you lead your company to maneuver, perform, and thrive in the new age we have now entered—The Age of Turbulence.

Philip Kotler
John Λ. Caslione
Chaotics: The Business of Managing
and Marketing in The Age of Turbulence
www.chaoticsstrategies.com

ACKNOWLEDGMENTS

We want to acknowledge the many influences on our thinking, starting with the father of management, Peter Drucker, and his book *Age of Discontinuity,* and to such other notables as Jim Collins (*Good to Great*), George Day and Paul Schoemaker (*Peripheral Vision*), Benjamin Gilad (*Early Warning*), Gary Hamel and C.K. Prahalad (*Competing for the Future*), Peter Schwartz (*Inevitable Surprises*), Peter Senge (*The Fifth Discipline*), Hermann Simon (*Hidden Champions*), and others.

We also want to acknowledge Ellen Kadin and her very supportive, patient, and dedicated team at AMACOM for all their assistance in guiding the creation of *Chaotics* and bringing it out on time.

Philip Kotler
John A. Caslione

Meeting the New Challenges

WHAT IS THIS book about? Those who manage businesses have a certain view of the world and a certain set of practices for dealing with expected changes in the marketplace. Their view, in the simplest terms, is that times are either normal as a precursor to runaway growth and sustained prosperity, or weak as a precursor to dwindling demand and possibly recession. Businesses use a different playbook for dealing with each of these market conditions. In normal times, they compete with a mixture of offensive and defensive plays, but are not likely to win big. In runaway growth periods, they see new opportunities everywhere. They invest and spend freely to capture what they can. In recession times, businesses cut their costs and investment to ensure their survival.

This view of two underlying market conditions, and two playbooks to guide the firm, is, however, outmoded. There are market conditions beyond these two basic ones. And conditions can suddenly shift from one to another and yet another. One day there is a 9/11 terrorist attack; another day, a Katrina flood. One day there is a panic about mortgages and defections that lead to a collapse of the world's financial system. Big shocks happen more frequently today as a result of an increasingly interconnected global economy supporting giant flows of trade and information.

The shocks come in all shapes and sizes. In many parts of the world, across many industries, important things are happening that are only dimly perceived if at all, and certainly their implications are not measured. It could be two people in a garage building a new gadget called a personal computer. It could be a guy named Jeff Bezos starting an Internet business called "Amazon." Or another guy named Steve Jobs building an iPhone. It could be a guy who envisions high yield bonds or another who develops the idea of securitizing mortgages. Had the computer industry, the book industry, the music industry, or the financial industry noticed these visionaries, they would have acted earlier to protect their turf or grab new opportunities.

Business leaders need a new view of the world and a new framework for dealing with it. According to this new view, change is occurring all the time. It can come quickly from any corner of the world and affect any company with a major impact. This is the view to which Peter Drucker first called our attention in his book *The Age of Discontinuity*.[1] This is the view that Andy Grove articulated in *Only the Paranoid Survive*.[2] This is the view that former U.S. Treasury head Alan Greenspan articulated in *The Age of Turbulence*.[3] This is the view that Clayton Christensen wrote in his *Business Innovation and Disruptive Technology*.[4]

It is our view as well that there is much more risk and uncertainty in business affairs today than ever before coming from disruptive innovations and big unexpected shocks. Business leaders have always lived with some risk and uncertainty, taking out insurance wherever possible to blunt the damage. But today, the speed of change and the magnitude of shocks are greater than ever. This is not what was normal in the past. This is the new normality. It goes beyond disruptive innovation to include major shocks.

And how are business leaders to deal with it? Because they must manage during times of greater turbulence, they need a system to make better decisions. They need a management framework and system to deal with chaos. They need a *Chaotics Management System.*

It seems everywhere in the world where we encounter business and government leaders, virtually everyone senses that *this time is different,* even if they cannot articulate precisely what makes it different. But as you'll see in Chapter 1, we often find an immediate acknowledgment and agreement when we explain to these leaders that they've entered into a *new normality,* one in which the days of the two cycles—one up and one down—are over for the foreseeable future. These leaders sense that we've entered an era of ongoing, continuous turbulence and heightened chaos. This realization is often accompanied by a sense of relief that they can now articulate what they've been sensing, coupled with dread that the traditional up cycle may not kick in to let the good times roll again—at least not like it did in the past.

It is for this reason that we wrote *Chaotics.*

In Chapter 1 we will identify the many factors creating this heightened turbulence demanding that business leaders need to reinvent their thinking to adopt new strategic behaviors to minimize their vulnerabilities and exploit their opportunities in the new normality.

In Chapter 2 we will explain why mistakes made by business leaders in past down cycles that, while they were not necessarily helpful to their businesses, in this new era they will be not only harmful but fatal to a business if it fails to adjust.

In Chapter 3, we will introduce the Chaotics Management System, which provides a roadmap for business leaders to transition their organizations, including adding new critical internal processes, to function successfully and better understand and deal with the events unfolding around them. By providing guidance in the development of early warning systems to detect turbulence in the environment, and constructing yet-foreseen scenarios and strategies, *Chaotics* will offer new and robust organizational muscle to handle the heightened levels of turbulence and chaos with decisiveness and speed.

In Chapter 4, we will describe new strategic behaviors necessary for each key management function in the organization to improve its short-term performance without jeopardizing its medium- and long-term performance.

In Chapter 5 we will provide a comprehensive roadmap to show how companies can sharpen and strengthen their marketing and sales strategies in turbulent times even when there's pressure to cut budgets in these areas, and to lay the groundwork for a stronger and longer future with a bigger and more loyal customer base.

And finally in Chapter 6, we will outline what business leaders can do to properly balance short-term with medium- and long-term demands of their businesses to preserve and build successful companies to live and thrive for many years into the future.

We are confident that *Chaotics* will provide business leaders the critical new insights, new perspectives, and a new system—including a set of new strategic behaviors and tools—to successfully navigate the unpredictable and uncertain waters in this new era, The Age of Turbulence.

CHAPTER ONE

The World Has Entered a New Economic Stage

From Normality to Turbulence

Prosperity is a great teacher; adversity a greater.
—William Hazlitt (1778–1830)

THE WORLD HAS entered a new economic stage. National economies are intimately linked and interdependent. Commerce is conducted with information flows moving at the speed of light over the Internet and mobile phones. This new stage confers wonderful benefits in bringing down costs and speeding up the production and delivery of goods and services. But it also comes with a dark side, one that substantially raises the level of risk and uncertainty facing producers and consumers. An event or change in the circumstances of one country—whether a bank failure, a stock market or real estate crash, a political assassination, or a currency default—can spread to many other countries and create massive turbulence, spinning the whole system toward completely unforeseen outcomes.

Deliveries don't arrive in time, banks stop making loans and start demanding repayment, employers lay off workers, and economies begin a downward spiral. Companies make more cautious decisions. They put new product development on hold; they reduce their marketing and advertising budgets. Prudence dictates slimming down, surviving in the short run and disinvesting as far as the long run is concerned. The great economist John Maynard Keynes remarked that in the long run, we are all dead.

Conditions eventually hit rock bottom, after a multitude of bankruptcies, foreclosures, lost jobs, and lost income. Somehow basic needs and government action may put a floor on the losses and things start looking a little better. Turbulence and pessimism are replaced by a measure of stability and renewed confidence. Betting on a recovery, some companies seek increased opportunities and investments. It all sounds like the classic business cycle with its ups and downs, where overexpansion is followed by subsequent underinvestment before returning to normal.

But even when normalcy returns to the economy, it doesn't return to every industry or market or individual company. Hypercompetition operates continuously and relentlessly in normal times. The U.S. auto industry today is experiencing a perfect storm of high health care costs and enormous pension obligations converging with falling demand for its products, which for decades have been seen as less attractive than foreign competitors' products. The airline industry is marked by too much capacity and further consolidation is likely. Even without a global financial meltdown, times can be turbulent for specific industries and organizations.

Turbulence always means an increase in risk and uncertainty. Risk is used to describe uncertainty that can be estimated and for which insurance can be purchased. But there is always uninsurable risk, real uncertainty that company decision makers face. Instead of companies seeking to maximize their returns in the face of high uncertainty, they might instead make decisions that minimize risk so that if the worst happens, the companies will still survive.

The National Intelligence Council released a 2008 report entitled *Global Trends 2025: A Transformed World*. Its purpose was to stimulate strategic thinking about the future by identifying key trends, the factors that drive them, where they seem to be headed, and how they may interact. It used a number of scenarios to illustrate some of the many ways in which the drivers examined in the report (e.g., globalization, demography, the rise of new powers, the decay of international institutions, climate change, and the geopolitics of energy) may interact to generate challenges and opportunities for future decision makers and business leaders. *Global Trends 2025* isn't a prediction of what is to come in the next decade and beyond, but a description of the drivers and developments likely to shape world events.[1]

Reading the report further reinforces the point that for the foreseeable future, the world will be facing ongoing disruptions, turbulence, chaos, and violence. These factors will impact business around the globe directly and indirectly, creating an environment that business leaders will have to deal with if their companies are to remain viable over the long term.

Such was the case in India over three terrifying days in late November 2008, when armed Islamist militants mounted a multipronged overnight attack in Mumbai, India's sprawling business capital of more than 18 million people. The sheer scale and audacity of the assault were staggering. Gangs of well-armed youths attacked two luxury hotels, a restaurant, a railway station, a Jewish center, and at least one hospital. Gunfire and explosions rang through Mumbai with 179 people killed and more than 300 wounded, including several foreigners from America, Japan, and

Britain, as well as Mumbai's chief counterterrorism officer. Up to 100 hostages, including selected American and British guests, were held hostage inside a hotel.[2]

The attacks appeared to ratchet up tensions in an already volatile region. As one of the BRIC countries (Brazil, Russia, India, and China, a term coined in 2001 by Goldman Sachs head of global research, Jim O'Neill), India was on the fast track to pull itself out of decades of economic stagnation before the terrorists hit. India, no stranger to terrorist attacks in recent years, had recovered from most of them to stay on its economic fast track. But regrettably, as the globalized world is now characterized by an interlocking fragility that spreads the news of chaos virally and instantaneously throughout a global news network, India, and possibly that entire region of Asia, may backslide. After all, foreign businesses are reluctant to put their people and their investments in harm's way.

As summarized in Figure 1–1 and Figure 1–2, there are a multitude of reasons for the rising uncertainty that will bring new and increasing challenges to business leaders in the next two decades.

In the next decade and beyond, according to *Global Trends 2025*, we can anticipate increasing turbulence around the world: rapid political leadership change in emerging markets; major policy shifts; increasing armed conflicts; local and national government budget cuts and the spillover effect on business. We are living in uncertain times. That means there is greater risk for businesses of all sizes everywhere in the world. They need new strategies to protect themselves and to capitalize on the opportunities that will undoubtedly arise.

While companies are gearing up for the greater turbulence and chaos that lie ahead, they will not soon forget the pain and the lessons of the 2008 financial meltdown. Companies will proceed more cautiously and adopt a risk-oriented mindset. Governments will try to pass regulations that will prevent a repeat of this kind

RELATIVE CERTAINTIES	LIKELY IMPACT
A global multipolar system is emerging with the rise of China, India, and others. The relative power of nonstate actors—businesses, tribes, religious organizations, and even criminal networks—also will increase. The unprecedented shift in relative wealth and economic power, roughly from West to East now under way, will continue. The United States will remain the single most powerful country but will be less dominant.	By 2025, a single "international community" composed of nation-states will no longer exist. Power will be more dispersed, with the newer players bringing new rules to the game, while risks will increase that the traditional Western alliances will weaken. Rather than emulating Western models of political and economic development, more countries may be attracted to China's alternative development model. As some countries become more invested in their economic well-being, incentives toward geopolitical stability could increase. However, the transfer is strengthening states like Russia that want to challenge the Western order. Shrinking economic and military capabilities may force the United States into a difficult set of tradeoffs between domestic versus foreign policy priorities.
Continued economic growth—coupled with 1.2 billion more people by 2025—will put pressure on energy, food, and water resources.	The pace of technological innovation will be key to outcomes during this period. All current technologies are inadequate for replacing traditional energy architecture on the scale needed.
The number of countries with youthful populations in the "arc of instability" will decrease, but the populations of several youth-bulge states are projected to remain on rapid growth trajectories.	Unless unemployment conditions change dramatically in parlous youth-bulge states such as Afghanistan, Nigeria, Pakistan, and Yemen, these countries will remain ripe for continued instability and state failure.
The potential for conflict will increase, owing to rapid changes in parts of the greater Middle East and the spread of lethal capabilities. Terrorism is unlikely to disappear by 2025, but its appeal could lessen if economic growth continues in the Middle East and youth unemployment is reduced. For those terrorists that are active, the diffusion of technologies puts dangerous capabilities within their reach.	The need for the United States to act as regional balancer in the Middle East will increase, although other outside powers—Russia, China, and India—will play greater roles than today. Opportunities for mass-casualty terrorist attacks using chemical, biological, or less likely, nuclear weapons, will increase as technology diffuses and nuclear power (and possibly weapons) programs expand. The practical and psychological consequences of such attacks will intensify in an increasingly globalized world.

Global Trends 2025: A Transformed World, U.S. Office of the National Intelligence Council, November 2008

Figure 1-1. *Global trends 2025: relative certainties and likely impact.*

KEY UNCERTAINTIES	POTENTIAL CONSEQUENCES
Whether an energy transition away from oil and gas—supported by improved energy storage, biofuels, and clean coal—is completed during the 2025 time frame. How quickly climate change occurs and the locations where its impact is most pronounced. Whether mercantilism stages a comeback and global markets recede.	With high oil and gas prices, major exporters such as Russia and Iran will substantially augment their levels of national power, with Russia's GDP potentially approaching that of the United Kingdom and France. A sustained plunge in prices, perhaps underpinned by a fundamental switch to new energy sources, could trigger a long-term decline for producers as global and regional players. Climate change is likely to exacerbate resource (particularly water) scarcities. Descending into a world of resource nationalism increases the risk of great power confrontations.
Whether advances toward democracy occur in China and Russia.	Political pluralism seems less likely in Russia, absent economic diversification. A growing middle class increases the chances of political liberalization and potentially greater nationalism in China.
Whether regional fears about a nuclear-armed Iran trigger an arms race and greater militarization. Whether the greater Middle East becomes more stable, especially whether Iraq stabilizes and the Arab-Israeli conflict is resolved peacefully. Whether Europe and Japan overcome economic and social challenges caused or compounded by demography. Whether global powers work with multilateral institutions to adapt their structure and performance to the transformed geopolitical landscape.	Episodes of low-intensity conflict and terrorism taking place under a nuclear umbrella could lead to an unintended escalation and broader conflict. Turbulence is likely to increase under most scenarios. Revival of economic growth, a more prosperous Iraq, and resolution of the Israeli-Palestinian dispute could engender some stability as the region deals with a strengthening Iran and a global transition away from oil and gas. Successful integration of Muslim minorities in Europe could expand the size of productive workforces and avert social crisis. Lack of efforts by Europe and Japan to mitigate demographic challenges could lead to long-term declines. Emerging powers show ambivalence toward global institutions like the UN and IMF, but this could change as they become bigger players on the global stage. Asian integration could lead to more powerful regional institutions. NATO faces stiff challenges to meet growing out-of-area responsibilities as Europe's military capabilities decline. Traditional alliances weaken.

Global Trends 2025: A Transformed World, U.S. Office of the National Intelligence Council, November 2008

Figure 1-2 Global Trends 2025: *key uncertainties and potential consequences.*

of housing and mortgage bubble. Banks and companies will be less prone to sell their goods and services "with no money down." Credit practices will be monitored more carefully to avoid another "house of cards" economy.

Intel's former chairman, Andy Grove, wrote in his best-selling book, *Only the Paranoid Survive,* that "strategic inflection points" occur in all businesses as a direct result of specific forces affecting particular businesses. A business has arrived at a strategic inflection point when its old strategy no longer works and must be replaced by a new one if the business is to ascend to new heights. If a company's leaders fail to successfully navigate their way through the inflection point, the business declines.[3]

Your instincts—or maybe your paranoia—will tell you to remain ever vigilant because you don't know when a strong and sudden wind will hurl your company or your whole industry into unwanted chaos. Sometimes the turbulence is minor. Other times it is more dramatic, such as when the great global financial meltdown of 2008 had nearly everyone gasping for breath as the markets experienced unpredictable and uncontrollable free fall from one day to the next.

Even more unsettling is the harsh recognition that whenever chaos arrives, you'll have little more than a fig leaf to hide behind—unless you can anticipate it and react fast enough to lead your company, your business unit, your region, or your department through it safely.

There's one more matter that makes leaders squirm: the increasing level of transparency that's now going to be demanded of you and your management team. Even if you and your company were merely victims of the global financial meltdown in 2008 that cost world shareholders in the real economy trillions of dollars of lost market value, your world and your company's world has now changed forever. The many institutional and private investor portfolios that lost up to half of their value in a matter of weeks—some of which include employees' pensions and savings plans—will now begin to demand a higher level of transparency from the companies in which they are invested. Scrutiny from all company stakeholders is already becoming increasingly intense. Going forward, more of your company's customers, employees, board directors, banks, suppliers, distributors, and the business and financial media overall will be watching your and other companies' actions a lot more closely to see how management runs their businesses at many levels.

What Is Market Turbulence?

To understand market turbulence and its effect on business, it may be helpful to review concepts of turbulence in nature as well as in science and physics. Turbulence in the natural world is characterized by violent or agitated behavior. Think of hurricanes, windstorms, tornados, cyclones, and tsunamis. Their defining characteristics are violence, randomness, and unpredictability.

Turbulence has always worried physicists because it is so difficult to model and predict, despite the sophistication and power of supercomputing today.[4] Scientists have developed Chaos Theory to study how events may unfold given an initial condition and deterministic assumptions. They can show that a small initial effect can lead to an exponential growth of perturbations. The behavior of dynamic systems—systems whose state evolves with time—appears random even though no randomness was built into the systems.[5]

On December 26, 2004, the great tsunami in the Indian Ocean that violently swirled in the air and the waters created tremendous turbulence and destruction in Asia. Although it wasn't physically felt by persons in San Francisco or in an airplane flying over Stuttgart, scientists have long postulated that, in fact, there is an effect in the atmosphere tens of thousands of miles away from the originating source. In 1972, Edward Lorenz, father of Chaos Theory, gave speeches in which he posed the question, "Does the flap of a butterfly's wings in Brazil set off a tornado in Texas?"

The phrase *butterfly effect* refers to the idea that a butterfly's wings create tiny changes in the atmosphere that may ultimately alter the path of a storm system like a tornado or delay, accelerate, or even prevent the occurrence of a tornado in a certain location. According to the theory, had the butterfly not flapped its wings, the trajectory of the tornado might have been vastly different. Scientists agree that the butterfly can influence certain details of weather events, including large-scale events like tornados.[6]

Now, you may ask, what does all of this have to do with turbulence in business?

To begin, business turbulence is defined as the unpredictable and swift changes in an organization's external or internal environments that affect its performance.[7] The "butterfly effect" occurs because ours is an increasingly interconnected, interdependent globalizing world that is accelerating in its "globalness." All people, all governments, all businesses—everyone and every entity in the world—are now connected and interconnected at some level, and the impact of the turbulence of each will be *felt* in some way by others in our globally connected environment.

To fully grasp the magnitude of the impact of turbulence—*severe turbulence*—and the resultant devastating chaos and wreckage that was left in its wake, we need look no further than the final four months of 2008, when several trillion dollars of market value in the real economy simply evaporated, leaving behind economic carnage for a newly elected U.S. president and the rest of the world to clean up and rebuild, globally.

In fact, the very public demise of investment bank Bear Stearns, dating back to March 2008, set the roller coaster in motion. After that, from September through October 2008, the world's stock exchanges were battered and torn. In early October, the S & P 500, the broad U.S. stock index, lost 22 percent of its value in just six trading sessions!

On September 24, 2008, U.S. Federal Reserve chief, Ben Bernanke, and then-Treasury Secretary Henry Paulson petitioned the U.S. Congress to support a $700 billion bailout plan (officially known as H.R. 1424: the Emergency Economic Stabilization Act of 2008). "Despite the efforts of the Federal Reserve, the Treasury, and other agencies," Bernanke told the lawmakers, "global financial markets remain under extraordinary stress."[8]

Ten days later, in an emergency meeting called by the heads of the four largest European economies to deal with the looming crisis, Jean-Claude Trichet, head of the European Central Bank, stated, "Nothing in the past resembles what we are currently seeing. We are in the presence of events that we have not seen since World War II. This is a period of absolutely exceptional uncertainty [that] calls for responses that match the events from both the public and private sector."[9]

The historic $700 billion bailout of the banking industry in the United States was matched by the European Central Bank's collective $1.3 trillion bailout of its banking industry, and followed by similar actions by central banks in Australia, Canada, Japan, Singapore, and many more countries. Hungary and Iceland lined up seeking rescue from the IMF, and others even sought direct help from cash-rich nations such as China and Russia.

But September 29, 2008, is the day that will live in financial infamy. That was when Wall Street ended a stunning session with a huge loss, with the Dow Jones industrials plunging more than 776 points in a matter of minutes—their largest point drop ever—after the U.S. House of Representatives failed to pass the bailout.

The credit markets remained close to frozen, as banks were afraid to lend, even to other banks. Eight consecutive days of losses erased an estimated $2.4 trillion in shareholder wealth. Conditions went from bad to worse. Borrowing costs for banks and companies jumped once again as investors sought safety in Treasury bills, despite earlier signs that the government might take equity stakes in troubled companies to try to halt the credit crisis. The cost of borrowing shot up for even blue-chip companies: IBM agreed to pay 8 percent interest on $4 billion of thirty-year bonds, twice the rate that the federal government borrows money. Then, on October 10, the roller-coaster ride abruptly ended when "the market made a U-turn, surging higher with the Dow climbing nearly 900 points in less than forty minutes."[10]

While the rebound momentarily allayed fears in the U.S., it set off a selling frenzy for the global financial community. Suddenly, previous boastful talk of nations decoupling from the U.S. economy seemed rather sardonic. Reports worldwide were grim. Global stocks had fallen sharply in one of the worst days of trading in thirty years, despite ongoing government efforts to stem the crisis.[11]

On October 24, 2008, when the world's stock exchanges dropped around 10 percent in most indices, Bank of England deputy governor Charles Bean warned, "This is a once-in-a-lifetime crisis, and possibly the largest financial crisis of its kind in human history."[12]

Between November 3 and 6, 2008, the U.S. Federal Reserve lowered interest rates to one percent; the Bank of England slashed its rate by 1.5 percent to 3 percent; and the European Central Bank cut rates to 3.25 percent, the lowest level since October 2006, and an aggressive response to the region's rapid plunge into recession.[13]

Then, on November 24, 2008, the U.S. government bailed out Citigroup Inc., agreeing to shoulder most of the potential losses on $306 billion of high-risk assets and inject $20 billion of new capital, in its biggest rescue of a bank yet.[14] And during the week of February 16th, 2009, U.S. President Obama signed his landmark $787 billion economic stimulus plan, in addition to his $75 billion housing stimulus package, in a bold effort to kickstart the U.S. economy and a key sector underpinning the stalled U.S. economy.

Since then, we continue to experience unpredictable, and also *heightened* turbulence in an increasingly globalizing world. Strategic inflection points will occur with increasing frequency, raising the stakes for all businesses to identify them more quickly and respond to the changed environment faster. The contrasts between normal business cycle times and turbulent economies are summarized in Figure 1–3: Normal Versus New Normality Economies.

FEATURE	NORMAL ECONOMY	NEW NORMALITY ECONOMY
Economic Cycles	Predictable	Absent
Upturns/Booms	Definable (Avg. 7 years)	Unpredictable, Erratic
Downturns/Recessions	Definable (Avg. 10 months)	Unpredictable, Erratic
Potential Impact of Issues	Low	High
Overall Investment Profile	Expansive, Broad	Cautious, Focused
Market Risk Tolerance	Acceptance	Avoidance
Customer Attitudes	Confident	Insecure
Customer Preferences	Steady, Evolving	Apprehensive, Flight to Safety

Figure 1–3. *Normal versus new normality economies.*

When we describe turbulence in the context of a *normal economy* versus a *new normality economy,* we need to better define what actually is a normal economy. Throughout the history of business there have always been levels of turbulence both at the macro level (the overall economy, whether it be local, regional, or global) as well as at the micro level, i.e., at the individual company level. Business owners and business people have always lived with certain levels of turbulence in the business. This is normal, and is part of a normal economy. And in the normal economy of the past, broad economic swings lasting several years were an essential feature. Over the past 50 years, we've come to count on two essential swings that mark a normal economy. First is the upswing that has historically lasted between six and seven years on average, oftentimes referred to as the "bull market." Second is the market downswing, lasting an average of ten months, often referred to as the "bear market", or sometimes as the "market correction."

These two swings were largely smooth and somewhat predictable in their movements, notwithstanding aberrations such as the stock market crash on October 19, 1987, a date that is also known as Black Monday. By the end of October 1987, all major world markets had declined substantially. It took only two years for the Dow to recover completely; by September 1989, the market had regained all of the value it had lost in the 1987 crash. During even these two years of recovery, while businesses would continue to battle competition as always, once the economic upswing began, it became substantially reliable—if not even substantially predictable—that the upswing would continue largely unabated and uninterrupted until such time as the next bear market correction would then kick in. Then the cycle would begin again.

Today's economy, with its heightened turbulence, is markedly different. Today and for the foreseeable future, the *new normality economy* is more than just normal times of up and down business cycles which, after all, has brought some predictability to businesses at the macro level. Today we can expect more big shocks and many painful disruptions, causing heightened levels of overall risk and uncertainty for businesses at both the macroeconomic and the microconomic level. On top of the everyday challenges of dealing in a perpetually competitive arena, and the usual business cycles, business leaders need to recognize a heightened stream of major and minor disturbances challenging their business planning.

The heightened turbulence is the *new normality* that challenges business and government leaders to better understand, fully accept, and then create new ways, new strategies to deal with it if we are to succeed in the years ahead.

Factors That Can Cause Chaos

Today's world of increasing interconnectivity and interdependence means more risk for every company. Critical factors that are raising the stakes for business risks include:

- Technological Advances and the Information Revolution

- Disruptive Technologies and Innovations

- The "Rise of the Rest"

- Hypercompetition

- Sovereign Wealth Funds

- The Environment

- Customer Empowerment

TECHNOLOGICAL ADVANCES AND THE INFORMATION REVOLUTION

Information technology (IT) is one of the key driving factors in the process of globalization. Advances since the early 1990s in computer hardware, software, telecommunications, and digitization have led to the speedy transfer of data and knowledge throughout the entire world. The information revolution is probably the single greatest contributor shaping the new global economy. Through the creation of interconnections with the potential to link all people and all businesses via a single medium—the Internet—the world's buyers and sellers can search, inquire, evaluate, and buy or sell from long distances. People no longer need to limit their buying or selling only to their local area.

Adding to the challenges for most business—especially large or legacy businesses—is that most of their top executives were born during the industrial revolution, but lead their companies during the digital revolution. In a sense, those over the age of thirty are *digital immigrants* and the "twentysomethings" are the *digital natives.* If anything, the information revolution has given way to information overload, which contributes to more turbulence and chaos.

The Internet has transformed and globalized commerce, creating entirely new ways for buyers and sellers to conduct transactions, for businesses to manage the flow of production inputs and to market their products, and for job recruiters and job seekers to connect with each other. New media have arisen—websites, e-mail, instant messaging, chat rooms, electronic bulletin boards, blogs, podcasts, webinars—creating a global system that makes it much easier for people and businesses with common interests to find one another, to exchange information, and to collaborate.

The global IT revolution has been driven by the extraordinarily rapid decline in the cost and rapid increase in the processing power of newer and newer digital technologies, doubling memory and computing power roughly every six months for the past two decades.[15] In the future, however, the single most powerful driver of the information revolution pushing globalization to even greater heights will be "cloud computing."

Cloud computing refers to the complex Internet-based infrastructure in which IT-related capabilities are provided "as a service." Users access "computing" services from the Internet "cloud" without needing knowledge of, expertise in, or control over the supporting technology infrastructure.[16]

As information technology embraces the global Internet "cloud," an increasing amount of computing activity is moving into data centers accessible from anywhere. IT is once again becoming more centralized. But how will that affect the way people conduct business?

The cloud will allow digital technology to penetrate every nook and cranny of the economy and of society, creating some tricky political problems and increased economic turbulence for businesses to deal with along the way. One theme is already emerging. Businesses must become more like the technology itself: more adaptable, more interwoven, and more specialized. These developments may not be new, but cloud computing will speed them up.[17]

Cloud computing services have been hugely successful with start-up businesses, which can now access and exploit software of the same quality found in large companies. Were it not for cloud computing services provided by firms such as Amazon.com and its Amazon Web Services (AWS) unit, many start-ups would probably not even exist. Take Animoto, a service that lets users turn photos into artsy music videos using artificial intelligence. When it launched on the popular social network Facebook, demand was so high that Animoto had to increase the number of its virtual machines on AWS from 50 to 3,500 within three days.[18]

The impact of Web-based services will be felt on a macroeconomic level, as cloud computing makes small firms more competitive with larger ones. And it will help developing economies compete with developed economies. These two factors alone will contribute greatly to increased market turbulence for companies of all sizes.

And the fact that the computing cloud is global will lead to political tensions over how it should be regulated. Cloud computing involves vast virtualized computer systems and electronic services that know no borders.[19] Governments will likely go to great lengths to avoid losing even more control over the Internet, which will invariably create further opportunities for turbulence and chaos for businesses that base their IT strategies more and more on cloud computing.

Regarding cloud computing, there is an underlying issue that few of today's experts have adequately addressed: knowledge sharing.

Technology to date has not solved the problem of finding people and sharing knowledge in an easy way. It is the proverbial "holy grail" and one that even Microsoft has not solved, although it tried to with SharePoint. Microsoft's SharePoint offering includes browser-based collaboration and a document-management platform that can be used to host websites that access shared workspaces and documents, as well as specialized applications like wikis and blogs, from a browser.[20] In fact, the real issue is to effectively—yet safely—*collaborate across firewalls and between companies* that are stakeholders in each other's business. The goal of sharing knowledge, while also limiting the sharing of too much knowledge (i.e., allowing access only to certain amounts of data), is still the biggest problem. The other remaining issue looming before business that has yet to be solved is that of *communication versus information.* This is, in fact, a false division because *information is communication* and *communication is information.* As long as software companies split these two worlds, however, the problem remains.

DISRUPTIVE TECHNOLOGIES AND INNOVATIONS

The term *disruptive technology* was created by Clayton M. Christensen, a Harvard Business School professor, who introduced it in his 1995 *Harvard Business Review* article, "Disruptive Technologies: Catching the Wave," and which he later described in his book, *The Innovator's Dilemma: When New Technologies Cause Great Firms to Fail.*[21]

In his later book, *The Innovator's Solution: Creating and Sustaining Successful Growth,*[22] Christensen eventually replaced the term *disruptive technology* with the new concept he called *disruptive innovation,* because he recognized that few technologies are intrinsically disruptive in character. The strategy or business model that the technology enables creates the disruptive impact. The concept of disruptive technology continues a long tradition of the identification of radical technical change. The great Harvard economist Joseph Schumpeter pioneered research on how radical innovations lead to "creative destruction" and are necessary for a dynamic economy.[23]

Disruptive technology, *or disruptive innovation, is a term describing a technological innovation, product, or service that uses a "disruptive"strategy, rather than an "evolutionary" or "sustaining" strategy, to overturn the existing dominant technologies or status quo products in a market. It has been systematically shown to the research community that most disruptive innovations are in a minority compared to evolutionary innovations, which introduce an innovation of higher performance to the market. Examples of true disruptive innovations are rare.[24]*

The entire basis of disruptive innovation is that it creates dramatic change in the market, causing the status quo technology to be quickly rendered obsolete. Such an event creates significant turbulence for all participants engaged in both the preexisting and the changed technologies. Some disruptive technologies on the five-year horizon include cloud and ubiquitous computing, contextual computing, virtualization and fabric computing, augmentive reality, and social networks and social software. Disruptive technology has the potential to be the ultimate "game-changer" that can create chaos in an entire industry, especially for the incumbents who haven't been paying attention to the turbulence quietly swirling around them until it is too late (see Figure 1–4).

Christensen distinguishes between "low-end disruption," which targets customers in a market segment who do not need the full performance valued by customers at the high end of the market, and "new market disruption," which targets customers who have needs that were previously unserved or insufficiently served.

Christensen postulates that "low-end disruption" occurs when the rate at which products improve exceeds the rate at which customers can adopt the new performance. Therefore, at some point the product's performance overshoots the needs of certain customer segments. Then, a disruptive technology may enter the market and provide a product that does not perform as well as the incumbent product but exceeds the requirements of certain segments, thereby gaining a foothold in the market.

DISRUPTIVE TECHNOLOGY/INNOVATION	DISPLACED/MARGINALIZED TECHNOLOGY
Mini steel mills	Vertically integrated steel mills
Container ships; containerization	"Break cargo" ships; stevedores
Desktop publishing	Traditional publishing
Digital photography	Chemical photography
Semiconductors	Transistors
Personal computers	Mainframes and minicomputers
Music downloads; file sharing	Compact discs
eBooks	Paper books
VoIP	Traditional telephones

Figure 1–4. Examples of disruptive technology/innovation.

Once the disrupter has gained a foothold in this customer segment, it will proceed to exploit the technology in order to improve its profit margin. Typically, the incumbent does little to defend its share in a not-so-profitable segment and usually moves up-market to focus on more attractive, profitable customers. The incumbent is eventually squeezed into smaller markets until the disruptive technology finally meets the demands of the most profitable segment, ultimately driving the incumbent out of the market entirely.

For example, early desktop publishing systems could not match high-end professional systems either in features or quality. Nevertheless, the early desktop publishing systems lowered the cost of entry to the publishing business, and economies of scale eventually enabled them to match, and then surpass, the functionality of older, dedicated publishing systems. As printers, especially laser printers, have improved in speed and quality, they have become increasingly competitive.

According to Christensen, "new market disruption" occurs when a product fits a new or emerging market segment that is not being served by existing incumbents in the industry. For example, when it was first introduced, the Linux operating system (OS) was inferior in performance to other operating systems such as Unix and Windows NT. But the Linux OS is inexpensive compared to others. After years of continuing improvements, Linux is now installed in 84.6 percent of the world's 500 fastest supercomputers.[25]

In disruptive technology battles, disrupters usually win against older technology incumbents in the industry. One reason is an asymmetry in financial incentives. A disrupter may see a huge opportunity, whereas the incumbent sees a much smaller one. Initially, the incumbent may actually find being disrupted even a bit pleasant, especially if the disruption causes the company's most unprofitable and troublesome customers to leave the market first. As its own profit margins improve, the incumbent may even be tempted to ignore the encroaching competition. The disrupter continues to make quiet innovations to its technology until it reaches a level sufficient to capture the core market from the incumbent.

Another reason disrupters usually win against incumbents is the fact that the larger, successful incumbent companies are organized into product divisions, whose managers will keep a close eye on their known rivals' offerings to ensure that their own products retain their edge. This inherent weakness of many incumbent companies is exacerbated by traditional silo behaviors within companies. Such behaviors occur not just between product divisions, but within each product division as well. The silos do not communicate: R&D doesn't communicate enough with design and development, production, marketing and sales, and business development. This silo effect has dire consequences and leads to the business operating like a slow-moving ship instead of a fast-moving speedboat. Collaboration across disciplines is essential. The disrupters, however, do not care about products as much as they care about those customers who aren't using the incumbent's products. The disrupters want to see what needs these potential customers have that are not being adequately fulfilled.[26]

When attacked by a disrupter, the first reaction by executives in incumbent technology companies is usually to protect their high-paying positions and their well-worn, comfortable business models. The typical response: *Close your eyes and maybe it will go away.* Occasionally it does go away, but usually it does not, and then the chaos really kicks in: Scramble to cut staff. Argue and debate. And make it as difficult as possible for the customer to actually adopt the new technology. Incumbents typically do everything in their power to put off the day of technological reckoning because their biggest problem is that they must bear the burden of supporting the older technology and the business model built around that technology, while at the same time experimenting with, building up, and transitioning into the new business model structures. Meanwhile, the technological disrupters do not bear this double-cost burden. For disrupters, everything is fluid and relatively low-cost.[27] And while the incumbents are fighting to make sense of the chaos in which they are so deeply mired, the disrupters are aggressively plowing forward with the winds and waves of turbulence at their backs.

Today, for instance, Microsoft may take comfort from the fact that Excel has more features than any other spreadsheet on the market.

On the other hand, a potential disrupter such as Google, with its Google Docs office suite, including its free Google spreadsheet, may take note that people are driven to despair when trying to transfer files from an old to a new computer, or that many Excel users cringe at the thought of paying Microsoft still more money to get the latest version of Excel.[28] If the disrupter's path is again repeated, Microsoft's current dominant position in spreadsheets could eventually give way to Google's free alternative.

THE "RISE OF THE REST"

A new chapter in global economic history has begun, one in which the United States, and to a lesser extent Europe, will no longer play their former dominant roles. A process of redistributing money and power around the world, away from the United States and Europe and toward the resource-rich countries and rising industrialized nations in Asia and the rest of the emerging world, has been under way for years. The financial crises of 2008 only accelerated the process.

Newsweek's Fareed Zakaria speaks eloquently about the new American malaise:

> American anxiety springs from something much deeper, a sense that large and disruptive forces are coursing through the world. In almost every industry, in every aspect of life, it feels like the patterns of the past are being scrambled. "Whirl is king, having driven out Zeus," wrote Aristophanes 2,400 years ago. And—for the first time in living memory—the United States does not seem to be leading the charge. Americans see that a new world is coming into being, but fear it is one being shaped in distant lands and by foreign people.[29]

What Zakaria calls the "rise of the rest" attests to the turbulence and the chaos caused by one of the most compelling new forces— the world's rising emerging market powers, most notably the BRIC countries (Brazil, Russia, India, China) and countries in the cash-rich Middle East. Zakaria writes further that the world is now entering the "third great power shift in modern history":

> The first was the rise of the Western world, around the fifteenth century, which produced the world as we know it now—science and technology, commerce and capitalism, the industrial and agricultural revolutions. It also led to the prolonged political dominance of the nations of the Western world. The second shift, which took place in the closing years of the nineteenth century, was the rise of the United States. Once it industrialized, it soon became the most powerful nation in the world, stronger than any likely combination of other nations. For the last twenty years, America's superpower status in every realm has been largely unchallenged—something that's never happened before in history, at least since the Roman Empire dominated the known world 2,000 years ago. During this "Pax Americana," the global economy has accelerated dramatically. And that expansion is the driver behind the third great power shift of the modern age—the rise of the rest.[30]

In the aftermath of the global financial crises that followed the simultaneous world stock market crashes in October 2008, China initially proclaimed itself relatively unscathed. Although as weeks progressed and the deep dependence of China's market on the United States and Europe became apparent, China's high-growth market quickly slowed. Chinese government leaders were forced to enact their own $585 billion economic stimulus plan. And then a few weeks later, in a bold showing of its new economic strength, when leaders of the world's top-twenty economies attended an emergency meeting in Washington to discuss reforming the world's financial markets and to gain commitments from the biggest economies to set aside money for a proposed International Monetary Fund (IMF) emergency loan fund for struggling countries, Beijing's delegates resisted calls for developing countries to contribute to the fund. Instead, China pushed for developing countries—itself especially—to have more influence at the IMF and other global bodies. Many analysts believe an increased say at the IMF may be Beijing's price to contribute funds. "Steady and relatively fast growth in China is in itself an important contribution to international financial stability and world economic growth," China's President Hu Jintao told state media at the summit.[31]

China, currently the world's third-largest economy with the biggest foreign-exchange reserves, also made no secret of its aspirations for a world financial order that's less dominated by the United States and its currency. With its $1.9 trillion in cash reserves, China, along with other Asia-Europe Meeting (ASEM) member countries, made plans to set up an $80 billion fund by the middle of 2009 to help countries in its own Asian backyard deal with liquidity problems—a plan already agreed to in May 2008 by ASEM.[32] And with the bulk of the money coming from China, it will have the ability to wield more clout.

BRIC countries and the Middle East are now stabilizing the global economy as consumption in these leading emerging market economies continues to offset the slowdown in the United States and Europe. During the turbulent months of 2008 when U.S. and European banks were sinking into a financial market tsunami, several leading financial institutions in Europe and the United States avoided bankruptcy when investments were made by various Middle East kingdoms and the Chinese government.

And while the number of companies from emerging markets appearing in the *Fortune* Global 500 rankings of the world's biggest firms continues to grow, the United States boasted only 153 in 2008, down from 162 in 2007—its worst performance in more than a decade.[33]

As Harold Sirkin writes in his book, *Globality: Competing with Everyone from Everywhere for Everything:*

> Imagine 100 companies from former Third World countries with a combined revenue in the trillions of dollars—greater than the total economic output of many countries—competing with U.S. and European companies for space on the world stage. Imagine several hundred such companies. Now imagine thousands. You are looking at the future, when U.S., European, Japanese companies, and companies from other matured markets will be competing not only with each other, but with Chinese companies and with highly competitive companies from every corner of the world: Argentina, Brazil, Chile, Egypt, Hungary, India, Indonesia, Malaysia, Mexico, Poland, Russia, Thailand, Turkey, Vietnam, and places you'd never expect.[34]

Companies from all these countries will be aggressively buying their way into the *Fortune* Global 500 with their acquisitions e.g. Budweiser of leading Western companies—juicy acquisitions with their experienced global and local management teams and their established global brands. Emerging market companies such as Brazil's Petrobras and InBev, Russia's Gazprom and Severstal, India's Reliance and Tata, and China's Lenovo and Huawei will increase turbulence and disruptions. These companies are growing at a record pace. The pace at which they acquire Western firms will increase as the global recession takes a bigger toll on companies in North America and Europe than on those in emerging economies. In fact, in 2008, the number of companies from emerging markets on the *Fortune* Global 500 list stood at sixty-two, mostly from the BRICs, up from thirty-one in 2003, and that number is set to rise rapidly. Based on current trends, emerging market companies will account for one-third of the *Fortune* list within ten years.[35]

Emerging markets companies will continue to capitalize on the chaos caused by the shifting balance of economic and political power in the world. These extremely ambitious and aggressive companies will do whatever it takes to beat competitors from developed economies, as it is in the developed economies where the most robust profits are found. These rising, globally aspiring upstarts from distant lands will do all that it takes to create as much chaos as necessary to trip up or buy up incumbents from the developed world to level the competitive playing field.

HYPERCOMPETITION

Hypercompetition occurs when technologies or offerings are so new that standards and rules are in flux, resulting in competitive advantages that cannot be sustained. It is characterized by intense and rapid competitive moves, in which competitors must move quickly to build new advantages and erode the advantages of their rivals. Speed of the disruptive turbulence created by hypercompetition is driven by globalization, more appealing substitute products, more fragmented customer tastes, deregulation, and the invention of new business models—all contributing to structural disequilibrium, falling barriers to market entry, and the dethronement of industry leaders.[36]

Richard D'Aveni, professor of business strategy at the Amos Tuck School at Dartmouth College and author of *Hypercompetition: Managing the Dynamics of Strategic Maneuvering,* argues that competitive advantage is no longer sustainable over the long haul. Advantage is continually created, eroded, destroyed, and recreated through strategic maneuvering by those firms that disrupt markets and act as if there were no boundaries to entry. The way to go about winning today is to render the current market leader's competitive advantages obsolete.[37]

Hypercompetition Strategies for Disruption

1. Stakeholder satisfaction is key to winning each dynamic interaction with competitors.

2. Strategic soothsaying is the process for seeking out new knowledge for predicting what customers will want in the future.

3. Speed is crucial to take advantage of opportunities and respond to counterattacks by competitors.

4. Surprise enhances a company's ability to stun a competitor, to build up superior position before a competitor can counterattack.[38]

Hypercompetition Tactics for Disruption

1. Signals sent to (1) make announcements of strategic intent to dominate a marketplace, or (2) manipulate the future moves of rivals.

2. Shift rules of the market to create tremendous disruption for competitors.

3. Simultaneous or sequential thrusts using several moves to mislead or confuse a competitor.[39]

In the age of turbulence, the competitive environment shifts dramatically from slow-moving incumbents attempting to protect their positions to fast-moving attackers with strategies targeted specifically at disrupting the competitive advantage of market leaders. These market leaders are often larger, inflexible firms with more traditional (and increasingly obsolete) competitive advantages. Competitive advantage becomes more transitory, and the most successful firms are those that migrate from one competitive position to another amid the turbulence and chaos.[40]

In the chaotic hypercompetitive environment, profits will be lower for firms that fail to create new competitive positions faster than their old positions crumble, especially as the weight of their depreciated and costly strategies will prevent many of them from adapting and adopting new chaotics behaviors fast enough.

SOVEREIGN WEALTH FUNDS

A sovereign wealth fund (SWF) is a state-owned investment fund made up of financial assets like stocks, bonds, property, precious metals, or other financial instruments. SWFs have been around for decades but have increased in number dramatically since 2000. Some are held solely by central banks that accumulate the funds in the course of managing a nation's banking system. This type of fund is usually of major economic and fiscal importance. Other SWFs are simply the state's savings, which are invested by various entities.[41]

During the global financial crisis in 2008, several U.S. and European financial institutions avoided bankruptcy by accepting SWFs from the Chinese government and various Arab kingdoms.[42] This says a lot about the "rise of the rest," as well as about who among those *rising* will be making waves in the new age.

In this new chapter in economic history, the perennial drivers of globalization over the past fifty years will no longer play their former dominant roles. A process of redistributing money and power around the world—away from the United States and Europe and toward the resource-rich countries and rising industrialized nations in Asia—has been under way for years following the 9/11 terrorist attacks, when China, Russia, the Middle East, and other rising economies began to accumulate tremendous hoards of cash as globalization gained momentum, and prices for oil, natural gas, and other commodities soared.

Sovereign wealth funds gained worldwide exposure in recent years by investing in several Wall Street financial firms, including

Citigroup, Morgan Stanley, and the former Merrill Lynch, when these firms needed a cash infusion due to losses at the beginning of the subprime mortgage crisis in January 2008. The tremendous damage that surfaced from the crises in late 2008 only accelerated the transformation process.

The wealthy state-owned investment funds of China, Singapore, Abu Dhabi, and Kuwait control assets of almost $4 trillion, and they are now, and for the foreseeable future, in a position to buy their way onto Wall Street and the major London and European exchanges in a big way, making big waves (see Figure 1–5).[43]

Most SWFs have remained cautious until now, partly as a result of poor experiences in the past. For example, China's China Investment Corporation invested $3 billion in the initial public offering of the private equity firm Blackstone Group in June 2008, and before that, $5 billion in Morgan Stanley in December 2007. In both cases, it lost a lot of money within months of its investments. Furthermore, the fall in oil prices has reduced the flow of cash into these funds.

But time may be on the side of the SWFs. With the long-term forecasts for severe recession in the United States and Europe

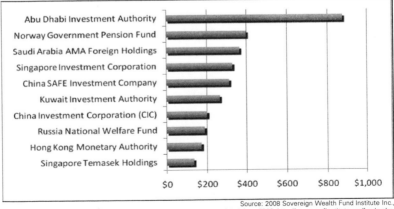

Source: 2008 Sovereign Wealth Fund Institute Inc., updated June 2008, http://www.swfinstitute.org/funds.php.

Figure 1–5. Top-ten largest sovereign wealth funds in 2008 ($ billion).

extending well into 2010,[44] U.S. and European stocks become cheaper each month, and American and European objections to buyers from Asia, Russia, and the Middle East become weaker as well. While the world is experiencing its global recession, moneys from these regions will be welcomed to help stabilize these Western economies.

Much of the turbulence eventually arising from SWF investments in these markets may come as a result of pent-up feelings of nationalism and protectionism. Before the many welcoming Western hands started reaching out, requesting SWF money to help stabilize their shaky financial markets, there was widespread skepticism from both the U.S. and many European governments. Such feelings date back to 2006, when the U.S. government rejected Dubai Ports World's proposed investments in several major U.S. seaports.

And the cynicism continued as more statements were made in mid-2008, when U.S. lawmakers and congressional investigators went on record stating that the unregulated activities of SWFs and other speculators have contributed to the dramatic swing in oil prices in recent months, and that the massive investment pools run by foreign governments are now among the biggest speculators in the trading of oil and other vital goods such as corn and cotton in the United States.[45] And then at the end of 2008, France's president, Nicholas Sarkozy, stated at a meeting of European leaders that Europe should have its own SWFs to take stakes in companies stricken by the global financial crisis to protect them from "predators," reasserting his previous promise to protect innocent French (and other European) companies from the "extremely aggressive" sovereign funds.[46]

Latent fears about incredibly wealthy—and opaque—sovereign wealth funds will add to the inevitable rise in protectionist sentiment when there is a return to less financially turbulent times. This rise in fear will be further fueled by the inherent disdain that many

Westerners have for oligarchic and state-led capitalism, both of which are prevalent in many emerging markets with the biggest SWFs.[47]

Ultimately, through corporate acquisitions and the investments of SWFs in the U.S., Europe, and other Western economies, the role of the state (often an undemocratic one) in the global economy is rapidly expanding, and with it the inevitable "push back" from Western governments and businesses, creating new sources of turbulence and chaos with which businesses will need to contend.

THE ENVIRONMENT

For many business leaders, when discussions turn to the environment, most often it conjures up the issue of risk and opportunity. In managing risk, very often a business's primary objective is to avoid the costs associated with an industrial accident, a consumer boycott, or an environmental lawsuit—all of which become more probable as the business climate becomes increasingly more turbulent. In managing opportunity, businesses must weigh the returns on their investments in the many opportunities they face every day.

All companies face increased pressure to conserve scarce natural resources and reduce pollution to ward off global warming so that life on the planet is not irreparably damaged. These requirements add to the cost of doing business overall, irrespective of any investment returns. The "green movement" is growing; it is gaining clout. Citizens and companies are entreated to consume and invest more conscientiously in systems that conserve air, water, and energy. And though most companies desire to support the green movement, with technological advancements it is becoming easier each year to prove that investments in environmental initiatives at the company level are actually bearing fruit, especially for shareholders. The potential for overinvestment is a real concern. Few companies in the post–global financial market meltdown have much discretionary money to invest on new projects that cannot directly deliver a solid return on the company's investment. Conversely, most companies now recognize that the growing markets for cleaner energy, water, food, transportation, and the like are already seeing bottom-line benefits from business strategies and innovation based on sustainable development. General Electric is one company trying to profit by providing solutions to energy and pollution problems.

Some investments in environmental initiatives are prudent and need to be seriously considered by companies, especially since stakeholders—who have environmental issues high on their list—increasingly express themselves about how businesses should be run. According to a *McKinsey Quarterly* survey conducted in September 2008, compared with one year earlier, many more executives said they now see environmental issues as opportunities rather than as risks. Executives answered questions on which issues matter most to the public. Environmental issues, including climate change, catapulted to the top of executives' sociopolitical agendas compared to the previous survey one year earlier. Around half of the 1,453 executives picked the environment as one of the top-three issues they expect will attract the greatest amount of public and political attention and most affect shareholder value.[48]

Because competitors are likely to invest in going green at different rates, at least in the short term, conditions favor those who skimp. In some markets, leveling the playing field may require more government regulation and enforcement. The overall effect will be to increase the level of turbulence within and across different industries. At first glance, the United States and Europe are likely to be competitively disadvantaged relative to less developed countries that are less able and less likely to make and enforce "green" investments. The West may try to use this as an excuse to lessen its own investments, leading to an ecologically risky outcome for everyone.

Ultimately, the value of companies is likely to change as environmental factors begin to affect their performance. The short-term impact on cash flows may be limited, but it will eventually be significant in some industries. As nations and companies begin acting more aggressively to address environmental concerns, including potentially expensive systems to reduce carbon emissions, major shifts in the valuations of sectors and companies will start to become clearer and more predictable. A critical first step is to review and quantify a company's exposure to noncompliance with current or prospective regulatory measures (such as carbon pricing, new standards, taxes, and subsidies), new technology, and environmentally prompted changes in customer and consumer behavior. Business executives will have to ask how specific changes would affect a company's competitive position if other companies adopted new business models and moved more quickly to going "green."[49]

To preempt any disruption or chaos prompted by environmental issue turbulence, the best companies will ultimately bring all stakeholders—both public and private—together to help shape the company's Business Enterprise Sustainability (BES) strategy so that environmentally effective "green" solutions also provide attractive returns on "green" investments.

CUSTOMER AND STAKEHOLDER EMPOWERMENT

In the past, businesses dominated the information airwaves. They would send out volleys of powerful brand messages on radio, TV, and billboards and in newspapers and magazines. If customers sought further information about a brand or a seller, they could only turn to their own experiences or to close friends and family members. Such "asymmetric" information was weighed in favor of the sellers.

In the last decade a revolution has occurred. Today's consumers continue to get advertising from sellers, but they also can survey hundreds of "friends" on Twitter, Facebook, or MySpace. They can look up reports online, on Angie's List, or Zagat, and learn what other businesses and people like themselves think of a company's products and services. Increasingly, each region or individual country around the world has its own new group of online, interactive sites connecting businesses and people to share experiences.

This means that customers and other stakeholders are no longer passive agents in the marketing process. They can learn as much about a company, product, or service as they choose. Beyond that, customers and all stakeholders can use what they have learned and tell others in their network by blogging, podcasting, e-mailing, or chatting.

"You cannot hide behind the curtain in this new world. Authenticity is key, and if there is any sign of lack of authenticity, the news is viral amongst the consumers . . . this is why service design is so bloody important," states Anna Kirah, a noted expert in innovation and concept making. "Understand that people look at a company as a service itself. People are buying the experience—not the product or service—and if the experience does not meet the expectation, the company will pay a high price." Kirah concludes, "Seeing this process holistically is crucial in the information revolution of today."[50]

The profound implication of this is that sellers who make substandard products or provide less than high-quality service will disappear faster than ever. The volume of word-of-mouth coming from businesses and people who have experienced a product or service will end up advertising the good guys and defeating the bad guys. And it will prod the good guys to get better and better. So customer and stakeholder empowerment acts as a catalyst leading to continuous improvement in the offerings of serious competitors.

By the same token, word-of-mouth has the potential to create turbulence and chaos for sellers. One person who experiences terrible service during a commercial flight can create a website devoted to the airline and welcome others with bad experiences to tell their tales. One angry customer or consumer can potentially undo an established company. Vigilant companies need to aim for high customer satisfaction and monitor the talk on the Internet to make sure that that one angry customer or consumer doesn't destroy the company. In today's world, one little angry voice has the potential to affect thousands.

British Airways and Virgin Atlantic are two examples of companies that were damaged by bad publicity through social networks—and paid the price. In October 2008, Virgin fired thirteen of its cabin crew who had posted derogatory comments about its safety standards and some of its passengers on a Facebook forum. Among other things, Virgin crew members joked that some Virgin planes were infested with cockroaches and described customers as "chavs," a disparaging British term for people with flashy bad taste. A few weeks later British Airways faced the same problem when it began investigating the behavior of several employees who had described some passengers as "smelly" and "annoying" in Facebook postings. While both airlines stated that they had policies prohibiting employees from posting such information online, and they had internal channels through which staff can vent frustrations, neither measure seemed effective enough to prevent employees from disparaging the companies publicly on the Internet.[51]

The Economist Intelligence Unit (EIU) performed a 2008 study that includes feedback from more than 650 enterprise executives, more than half holding C-suite titles. The study shows that a key driving force for change is the technology-enhanced interaction between employees, suppliers, investors, and most important, customers. The data also shows that over the next five years, e-mail via fixed and mobile devices will solidify its position as the most important communication channel for establishing and maintaining strong online business interactions with these audiences. Among the highlights from the EIU study:[52]

■ E-mail (according to 93 percent of respondents) and the World Wide Web (81 percent) maintain their leading positions as preferred business communications channels, and will continue to do so through 2013.

■ There will be a general increase in adoption across other emerging "networked" channels by 2013 to enable companies to build new competencies in-house and collaborate with outside partners.

■ Customer empowerment through technology will have a profound and positive effect on business. More than 76 percent of respondents believe this empowerment will positively impact new product and service development, and 73 percent expect that it will have a positive influence on revenues.

■ Organizations believe that the most significant impact on their business models between today and 2013 will be as a result of technology-led operational changes.

■ Executives anticipate technology changes will considerably affect their companies' customer service (40 percent of respondents) and sales and marketing (24 percent) initiatives, which rely heavily on e-mail and Web communications.

And in the face of the quickening pace of technological and social change, e-mail is becoming the new "snail mail." Traditional companies are less likely to recognize this fast enough and will lose out to those who adopt the faster communication media. The Internet and the World Wide Web enable communication and collaboration between empowered consumers and the businesses with whom they choose to engage. As customers increasingly demand greater input into how businesses interact with them, leading organizations of all sizes will gain advantages by transforming this increased customer involvement from risk to opportunity and long-term success.

Conclusion

Having reviewed the main factors causing change and turbulence, businesses must recognize that they cannot operate as they have in the past, with one playbook for normal and boom markets and another for down and recessionary markets. Today, businesses in all markets must be able to manage and market in environments exposed to some level of turbulence. What's needed now is *a new strategic framework for operating in the face of intermittent and unpredictable turbulence.*

When he wrote of turbulence during the deep recession in the early 1990s, Peter Drucker stated:

> In turbulent times, an enterprise has to be managed *both* to withstand sudden blows and to avail itself of sudden unexpected opportunities. This means that in turbulent times the fundamentals have to be managed, and managed well.[53]

Turbulence is occurring at a blistering pace, leaving many businesses unprepared and vulnerable to the chaos it brings. Entering this new era is a time of tremendous opportunity, but also one of substantial risk. And while turbulence in business cannot be avoided, companies can certainly choose how they will face it. They can navigate through the turbulence or be caught up in it. They can ignore or resist turbulence's chaos while trying to hold on and survive, or they can anticipate and leverage the forces of turbulence to their advantage.

Businesses must now develop the skills, the systems, the processes, and the disciplines to quickly detect and predict turbulence in their environment and identify the vulnerabilities and opportunities that come from the consequent chaos—and the business enterprise must respond wisely and deliberately and with strong resolve.

We wrote *Chaotics* with this very purpose in mind. In *Chaotics,* we share our insights and our observations of companies that have confronted turbulence and heightened turbulence, and what they've done to survive better than their competitors. We present guidelines for developing early-warning systems to recognize *weak signals* that may offer only *soft cues* to detect and predict turbulence that are missed by most companies. We describe scenarios for imagining what could happen as a result of different new forces. We consider responses to each scenario that would avoid or minimize the damage. We introduce methodologies and checklists in Chapter 3 for designing *Chaotics Management and Marketing Systems* to help create a robust and resilient business enterprise that capably manages risk and uncertainty and skillfully exploits opportunities during chaotic times.

Chaotics presents a disciplined approach to detecting sources of turbulence, predicting consequent vulnerabilities and opportunities, and developing critical and appropriate responses to ensure that the business lives on successfully and thrives. The aim is to achieve Business Enterprise Sustainability (more about that in Chapter 6).

All business leaders are intensely focused on creating strategies, organizational structures, and company culture to create "superior customer value" over the life of a business enterprise. In the age of turbulence, maximizing the creation of value on an ongoing and continuous basis will require a new set of behaviors.

In *Chaotics,* we are not advocating a conservative, risk-avoiding approach to strategy, but rather an alert and prudent approach that both protects the business enterprise from the disruptive forces that impact businesses during times of turbulence and yet advances its interests. It is a prophylactic approach to business risk, one that wards off the likelihood of hubris and greed overtaking the more sober management of business affairs.

We see *Chaotics* as providing business leaders across a wide range of industries with a single source handbook they can use to prepare their companies to face the chaotic situations that lie ahead, and succeed in The Age of Turbulence.

CHAPTER TWO

Management's Wrong Responses to Turbulence Now Become Dangerous

Be fearful when others are greedy, and be greedy when others are fearful.
— Warren E. Buffett, CEO, Berkshire Hathaway, Inc.[1]

THE ONE ABSOLUTE truth about the uncertainty that turbulence creates is that the longer it persists, the more cautious people become. When businesses are unable to predict their customers' expectations, they tend to abandon their core principles. The result is a very dangerous combination of turbulence pushing the stable footing out from underneath the most sound and respected companies while compromising a business leader's ability to make sound decisions.

Executives should strive to make their operations more efficient and to reduce unproductive expenditures, especially in areas that show signs of bloat—regardless of the business conditions. Let's be honest: Discipline tends to slip during a lengthy upturn in the economy, such as the one that has occurred in recent years.

Too often, here's what happens: Business executives approach impending trouble with overconfidence, often denying that their industry or their companies face any real danger. Then, when the downturn is an established fact, they make across-the-board cuts. They cut everything, from marketing and R & D spending to employee head count. Finally, when signs of recovery are everywhere, they open up the spending dam to show their strength and rebuild morale. Although these approaches seem reasonable in the heat of the moment, they can eventually damage competitive positions and financial performance. In The Age of Turbulence, this damage can be irreparable.

The fact of the matter is this: Economic uncertainty is like an elixir that can lead even the most skilled of CEOs, when they fall under its influence, to make serious mistakes. When panic spreads and peaks, many business leaders retreat. They slash costs in all the wrong places. They fire talent, shy away from risk, cut back on technology and product development, and worst of all, they let fear dictate their decisions. This action will not only hinder but can even destroy a company.

Battening down the hatches is not the only way to ride out a storm, just the most predictable one—and not necessarily the one that has the best interest of the company at the forefront. To be frank, turbulence in the business world leads to all the wrong responses from management. Many businesses and their executives subscribe to one of two conventional approaches to turbulence and the resulting chaos: They take few (if any) precautions, acting as if the storm will blow over, or else they run for cover, either slashing costs or, desperately caught in "magical thinking," investing in new and often unrelated businesses to hedge their bets.

While most business executives seem to dread a recession, not Michael O'Leary, the CEO of Ryanair, the biggest budget airline in

Europe. "We love recession," O'Leary said in an interview in the midst of the airline industry going into a tailspin in November 2008. "The best outcome for us this winter is a good, deep recession."[2]

The founder and CEO of Europe's other major low-cost airline (and Ryanair's fiercest challenger) did not share that view. The divergence between Ryanair and easyJet was highlighted during a recent period of overall uncertainty for the airline industry when, during the same week, O'Leary announced a dramatic plan to expand Ryanair while easyJet's Stelios Haji-Ioannou urged his management team to adopt exactly the sort of caution that O'Leary was throwing to the wind.

O'Leary sees economic downturns pressuring weaker carriers to cut routes, allowing his airline to move in. He also sees the opportunity for Ryanair to benefit during a downturn from falling jet fuel prices, declining labor costs, and the possibility of cash-strapped rivals reneging on orders for new planes. So as the recession landed in Europe and other airlines shrank and merged, O'Leary's expansion plans lifted off, with O'Leary claiming Ryanair could double its profit and its passenger numbers by 2012, despite signs that short-distance air traffic was declining.[3]

In October 2008, against the backdrop of Ryanair's bold moves, one of the fast risers on Europe's low-cost airlines scene, Sterling Airlines, went bankrupt after its Icelandic owner ran out of money—seemingly overnight—adding Denmark's second-largest carrier by fleet size to a list of more than two dozen carriers around the world to cease operating that year.[4]

Only those courageous few, like Ryanair's O'Leary, are willing to swim against the current and defy conventional wisdom. This gives them the greatest chance to place their companies in the strategic position to gain market share and grow shareholder value. The best executives resist any such desperate extremes by preparing for the worst while focusing on what their companies do best. Chaos has a way of giving an advantage to those who find opportunity in the present circumstances—whatever those circumstances are. This, essentially, is what we can affectionately term as chaos's own process of natural selection, in which it is decided which businesses will emerge as winners and losers. Companies that are on top today may not be on top tomorrow, and vice versa.

In fact, according to management consulting firm McKinsey & Company, almost 40 percent of leading U.S. industrial companies toppled from the first quartile of their sectors during the 2000–2001 recession. A third of leading U.S. banks met the same fate. But at the same time, 15 percent of companies that were not industry leaders prior to the recession vaulted into that position during it.[5]

These can be dangerous times for all management. Even when a company seemingly does everything right, it can still be swept away by the turbulence that others close to them cannot resist. Goldman Sachs, the premier global investment banking and securities firm, once considered unsinkable, found itself grabbing for the life preserver as American International Group Inc. (AIG) started sinking and sucking its clients down with them. (For more on the Goldman Sachs story, see the sidebar.)

GOLDMAN SACHS: A CASE OF RISK VERSUS UNCERTAINTY[6]

No one in the corporate world imagined, let alone predicted, the forced takeover of Bear Stearns, the conservatorship of Fannie Mae and Freddie Mac, the failure and rescue of AIG, the bankruptcy and sale of Lehman Brothers, the sale of Wachovia to Citibank and then to Wells Fargo, and the takeover of Countrywide by Bank of America—all of which occurred in a matter of months in late 2008. The global economy received a healthy dose of the surreal, and in the process, even these seemingly unstoppable business institutions have come undone.

And perhaps the most shocking fallout from this turbulent crisis stems from reports that Goldman Sachs would have suffered a loss of $20 billion on its counterparty credit risk with AIG had the

U.S. government not stepped forward and bailed out the global insurance giant from its liquidity crisis.

Before all hell broke loose, Goldman was considered immune to the woes of the rest. In 2007, when the subprime disaster hit, Goldman Sachs was "increasingly perceived as the world's biggest hedge fund." While other financial institutions were licking their wounds, Goldman was proudly boasting of its success. So how did it succeed where everyone else failed?

The bank made no secret of its success in its 3Q08 report of September 20. "Net revenues in [trading] mortgages were . . . significantly higher, despite continued deterioration in the market environment. Significant losses on nonprime loans and securities were more than offset by gains on short mortgage positions." Put another way, Goldman Sachs cleaned up during the collapse in subprime mortgage bonds in summer 2008 . . . by selling the subprime mortgage-backed market short.

As the story goes, the head of risk management at Goldman Sachs identified the risk of mortgage-backed securities (subprime) early on and raised the alarm to Goldman's executive board. He made his recommendation to sell off as much of the potentially "toxic" securities as he could, and for those that he couldn't sell, he secured insurance against their risk with a reinsurer.

Goldman seemingly did *everything* correctly, and yet it still got into deep trouble during the subprime crisis. Why? The risk was laid off to AIG, which couldn't cover its insurance commitments to Goldman, nor to anyone else. AIG needed rescuing from the U.S. government to the tune of $143.8 billion in loans and funding with a lot more on the way from the federal bailout funds. It was an enormous amount—nearly twice the expected amount when the original loan was advanced, to the shock of many. And by mid-March 2009, AIG reported their prior quarter's financial results shocking everyone with a record-setting loss of $61.7 billion—the largest of any company in the U.S. (or the world) for one quarter, while the U.S. government estimated that

AIG might need an additional $250 billion of U.S. taxpayers' money to further shore up its financial position.

The lessons here are two: First, risk is measurable, so it is insurable, while uncertainty is not. And second, in this new world of ever-increasing interdependencies and interconnectivity, even when a company—any company, in any industry, in any country in the world—behaves with foresight and does so both prudently and capably, any one of its shareholders can create turbulence in its business that has the potential to bring down that business, and bring it down hard and fast.

The only assurance that chaos can provide to even the most successful management team is that there are no assurances in times of turbulence, and especially heightened turbulence. This is why as chaos reigns more frequently and unpredictably, management must be more aware of and adeptly ready to avoid the most common mistakes businesses make when turbulence hits, and they must navigate through it (see Figure 2–1).

Some companies emerge from turbulence stronger and more highly valued than they were before the turbulence hit. By making

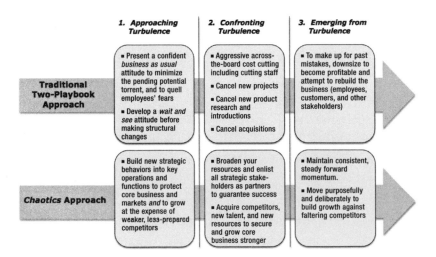

***Figure 2–1.** Navigating turbulence.*

strategic choices that sometimes defy traditional wisdom, they increase their stock market valuations relative to those of their former peers and gain more power to shape their industries.

Now let's turn our attention to some of the most common mistakes that business leaders make when turbulence hits:

- Resource allocation decisions that undermine core strategy and culture

- Across-the-board spending cuts versus focused and measured actions

- Quick fixes to preserve cash flow, putting key stakeholders at risk

- Reducing marketing, brand, and new product development expenses

- Declining sales and price discounting

- Decoupling from customers by reducing sales-related expenses

- Cutting back on training and development expenses in economic crises

- Undervaluing suppliers and distributors

Resource Allocation Decisions That Undermine Core Strategy and Culture

Every company faces difficult choices, especially when the economy tightens or, worse yet, grinds to a halt. But during times of turbulence, the decisions a leader makes will be even more far-reaching. There will be a lasting and significant impact not only on the bottom line but on employees, morale, and the culture and values that define the company, particularly if the decision undermines the company's fundamentals and fails to meet customers' expectations.

An excellent case in point is Home Depot. When Bob Nardelli was CEO of Home Depot in 2000, he didn't seem to have a passion for the heart and soul of Home Depot at all. While he clearly made interventions that were absolutely necessary, ranging from establishing a more rigorous strategy process to bringing the company's IT infrastructure up to state-of-the-art standards, he seemed to overlook what made Home Depot a cherished partner to the do-it-yourselfers and contractors who formed the core of its customer base.

The original Home Depot strategy depended on extremely knowledgeable service staff who would go that extra mile for customers and who could really help them understand how to accomplish their own goals. In the name of efficiency, Nardelli cut coverage, replaced quite a number of the experienced old-timers with less-experienced employees, and put the whole organization on a tight, numbers-driven, almost military program. Again, many of his changes were for the better—yet the cultural, network, and experience losses eventually caught up with the company and Nardelli was replaced.[7] (Nardelli later became CEO of Chrysler, LLC and was in that post during the 2008–2009 federal government bailout of the U.S. auto manufacturers.)

The moral of this story: Never lose sight of your company's core values. Undermining the culture and reallocating resources can have long-term damaging effects. Not only can it weaken the fundamentals of the company, but—as was the case with Home Depot—it may tarnish its brand.

Additionally, in an article entitled "Is Your Growth Strategy Your Worst Enemy?" McKinsey consultants wrote, "Withdrawing resources from inefficient processes may ultimately raise costs rather than lower them. Managers are frequently tempted to save money by reallocating resources, but this seldom works unless all of the interwoven processes involved are improved at the same time." The authors go on to note that:

Resource limitations set up a spiral of shrinking effectiveness. Say I buy a car because my dealer assures me that the current incentive scheme is about to end. Ten days later, I discover that the program has been not only extended, but enhanced. I have every right to be annoyed. If customer dissatisfaction becomes widespread, promotions will falter, leaving a shortfall in auto sales that the OEM may try to make up by introducing more "sweeteners"—the source of the discontent in the first place. Promotional spending then hits budget limits and incentive programs are curtailed to save money, becoming still less effective. Sales fall short once more, and the downward spiral feeds on itself.[8]

The harsh reality is that companies will need to cut costs somewhere when the economy is down, and there are times when a company's very survival demands dramatic cuts which absolutely must be made to save the company. But it's essential that cost-saving measures do not impair the company's uniqueness quotient, fall short of customer needs and expectations, or place the culture and values in peril. In the end, Shakespeare's advice, "To thine own self be true," applies to today's businesses that are experiencing turbulence.

Across-the-Board Spending Cuts Versus Focused and Measured Actions

When written in Chinese, the word crisis is composed of two characters. One represents danger and the other represents opportunity. These characters could easily symbolize the perils that await a company that makes across-the-board spending cuts versus those that are laser-focused on assessing where to make measured cuts. Management needs to keep its eye on the end goal, which is to emerge as a leader once the market returns—and this is rarely, if ever, the case when management resorts to across-the-board cuts.

Management's decisions—right or otherwise—during times of turbulence and chaos will determine the fate and position of a company when the economy makes its upswing. Diamond Management & Technology Consultants published a report in November 2008 entitled "Don't Waste a Crisis: Lessons from the Last Recession." They found that 48 percent of the companies that cut expenses across the board during the last major recession either lost ground or remained an also-ran. However, more than half of the companies actually increased gross margins during the recession year of 2001 and by the end of the recession had improved margins by an average of 20 percent. John Sviokla, Diamond's managing partner of innovation and research, observes: "Our research reveals that at the very time when leaders are tempted to shorten their time horizon and make arbitrary across-the-board cuts, superior performers dig into the data about their company performance and outsmart the competition." Sviokla goes on to say that "everyone cuts costs, but doing so in a way that improves the design and performance of the business separates the winners from losers."[9]

The Diamond study further found that companies generally fall into one of four categories based on how they enter and how they emerge from an economic downturn. "Stalwarts" are those consistently high performers that ranked within the top quartile among their industry peers both before and after a recession. Companies identified as "Opportunists" rebounded from a recession and improved their financial performance by 10 percent or more when compared to the financial performance of their industry peers. On the other end of the ratings, companies called "Low Idlers" show little if any significant difference in performance regardless of economic conditions. And, finally, those companies termed "Disappointed Stars" typically suffer worse financial performance when compared to all others surveyed after they emerge from a recession. These companies tended to lose 10 percent or more compared to their industry peers.[10]

Many leaders feel damned if they do and damned if they don't make cuts in turbulent times. Where do you cut? How deep? Or should you increase spending? And what will be the net effect of these decisions? What would Warren Buffett do? If only the "Oracle of Omaha" could give every manager the right answer.

At the Erin Anderson B2B Research Conference at the Wharton School, held in October 2008, Gary Lilien, a professor and research director of Penn State's Institute for the Study of Business Markets, was asked whether firms should increase spending during a recession. His answer:

> Everybody's looking for a single answer to a question that actually has multiple answers. We actually did some research on a [related] topic. It does depend. The firms that have what I call "the skill, the will, and the till" should, in fact, increase their spending and focus on acquiring new customers while retaining existing customers. "The skill" means they have marketing expertise. "The will" means they have a culture to go against what seems to be a tough trend. And "the till" means that they have some resources to be able to invest. The analogy is, the best athletes often attack at the toughest times on a hill. What if you don't have those assets? Now is the time to be focused on retaining existing customers.[11]

Turbulence, and the resulting chaos it brings, places every company in a different situation—some with greater risk than others—when it comes to finances and overall liquidity. And as Lilien suggests, there is no one-size-fits-all strategy. This is why it is essential to avoid across-the-board cuts and instead look for measured and focused cuts. To do this, management needs to ask the tough questions: How did we perform during the last recession? What did we learn from our performance? What is our liquidity situation? Do we have a roadmap that assessed our past performance? Does it take into consideration the mayhem and uncertainty that economic turbulence has caused? And will this roadmap take us to the future?

Again, companies need to view themselves as primarily service providers. A company's service is the combination of its identity—that is, its brand, its organization, and the products it sells. If any of these are broken, service is broken, and so is the company's value proposition. So, when looking at measured and focused cuts, companies need to keep in mind how any cuts they make affect the different aspects of the business so that their value propositions are not compromised.

Again, it all comes down to management's willingness to ask the tough questions: Where do we want to be positioned once the economy is on the upswing? Do we want to be among the elite quadrille that continues to grow and increase its market share? Or will we number among the casualties—the stalled and low-performing companies that made all the wrong decisions?

Quick Fixes to Preserve Cash Flow, Putting Stakeholders at Risk

Key strategic mistakes may become expensive when companies look for quick fixes to preserve cash flow. Being profitable is the endgame; every decision has to be weighed against its effects on cash flow. But when quick fixes are made to deal with the here and now, management risks jeopardizing the company's future growth.

Cutting staff, unnecessarily selling off assets, decreasing M&A activities, and slashing investment in R&D can set a company up for a hard landing.

Across-the-board staff reductions are always a mistake. Because of U.S. accounting laws, investments in talent are expensed, not capitalized, so cutting back on people, especially smart, high-priced people, is a quick way to cut costs. The accounting rules only hurt companies that follow them. Talent is the single most important variable in innovation.[12]

When a company cuts loose its talent, there is a greater chance its competitors will hire that very same talent the next day to help position themselves for better financial days and to help drive innovation in the interim. These times of uncertainty bring out predatory instincts in business leaders—as they should. Consequently, many companies are just waiting for the opportunity to use this time to hire key individuals they might not have been able to lure away during an economic boom.

Moreover, as recovery comes, the scarce resource for most companies will be talent, not capital. Many management teams thought they could win the war for talent during the 1990s boom by throwing stock options and perks at their employees and letting employees wear jeans to work. When the downturn came, there was an abrupt shift from "we value talent" to "you are a disposable cost." The options evaporated, the perks were withdrawn, and the layoffs came swiftly—in some cases, brutally. This tore the social fabric of many firms and left employees cynical.[13]

Management that doesn't understand or embrace the value of the talent that creates and drives the company's innovation will be hovering with the other stalled companies at the bottom of the business food chain.

Reducing Marketing, Brand, and New Product Development Expenses

When it comes time to make cuts, marketing always seems to get the first swipe, and new product development the second. This is always a mistake because it destroys market share and innovation.

The knee-jerk reaction from most companies is to cut marketing. When you cut marketing, you are leaving room for your competitors to get their message out in the forefront and to gain greater market share as yours slips away.

During times of turbulence, the most important thing is to stay alert and focused. Avoid committing the three biggest marketing mistakes that companies often make:[14]

1. *Stretching to Attract New Customers Before You've Secured the Core.* Trying to broaden your core product or service appeal to please a wider audience is risky. Chances are that you will make your best and most loyal customers even less satisfied, giving them one more reason to consider your competitors.

2. *Cutting Marketing.* Marketing dollars in weak or turbulent economies are like water in the middle of a dry desert—the less there is, the more valuable the amount you possess becomes. Cutting your marketing spending is guaranteed to give your more aggressive competitors who don't cut budgets the edge they need to take away your most valued customers. Marketing is muscle, not fat.

3. *Neglecting the 900-Pound Gorilla.* We live in a 24/7 world of nonstop information. When news breaks, everyone gets it, including your customers. During down markets, especially when turbulence and chaos reign, your customers and all of your company's stakeholders know that business isn't great. Ignoring this fact and, worse, not keeping them updated is dangerous.

Failing to invest in product development is guaranteed to hinder future value creation for the company and its stakeholders. When companies neglect or reduce the importance of product development in an effort to save money, it not only limits potential growth, but it curbs innovation and gives competitors who've taken the risk the upper hand.

BusinessWeek compiled a list of the ten worst mistakes made by companies that are trying to cope during a slowing or turbulent economy. The list reminds management that unless you really want to compete on price (remember, India launched its $2,500 Nano car), the ability to do sustained innovation is one of the few ways left to maintain a competitive edge and to separate yourself from your competitors. Innovation drives performance, growth, and stock market valuation.[15]

Top-Ten Innovation Mistakes a Company Can Make During a Turbulent Economy

1. Fire talent.

2. Cut back on technology.

3. Reduce risk.

4. Stop product development.

5. Allow boards to replace growth-oriented CEOs with cost-cutting CEOs.

6. Retreat from globalization.

7. Allow CEOs to replace innovation as key strategy.

8. Change performance metrics.

9. Reinforce hierarchy over collaboration.

10. Retreat into walled castle.

It is natural for companies to be more conservative when there are budgetary concerns, but companies that don't take risks, don't invest in product development, and misjudge the need for collaboration will find it difficult to compete when the market is on the upswing.

Companies that invest in R&D and new product development when times are tough, on the other hand, will continue to make money. In fact, more than merely continuing to make money, they will be winners that always emerge out of the most difficult economic times and almost always beat their competition on the basis of something new. For example, Apple worked on iTunes, the iPod, and its retail stores during the 2001 recession and was perfectly positioned to roll over its competition once growth returned.

Another example is Gillette, which launched its Sensor brand of shaving products mid-recession in the early 1990s. By 1997, 49 percent of Gillette's sales came from new products introduced in the previous five years.

Or Intel, which invested 14 percent of sales (a whopping 174 percent of 2001 profits) during the 2001 recession on innovations to produce faster, cheaper, smaller computer chips. Intel went on to launch new products months ahead of schedule and reported its highest growth rate since 1996.[16]

Apple, Gillette, and Intel didn't make any of the top-ten innovation mistakes a company can make during a turbulent economy. Your company shouldn't either.

One of the keys to working your way through turbulence is to adapt to a tough mindset. In tough times, pragmatism rules. As business results sour, it will be tempting to blame a tough economic environment. But even in the toughest of times, some competitors outperform others. The only way to come out a winner in the turbulence ahead is to seize the moment: Make hard-nosed, practical decisions that will give your company and your products a fighting chance to survive—maybe even to thrive.

Declining Sales and Price Discounting

The pricing paradox is one the biggest pitfalls that management has to deal with during an optimal economy. But pricing can be management's worst nightmare when the economy goes south and sales begin to slide. Price discounting is always a risk, but when done incorrectly it can have ominous and paralyzing effects on a business.

A case study in progress is Starbucks Coffee. Its 3Q08 profits were down 97 percent in November 2008, while its newest competitor, McDonald's, found a way to thrive during these times. McDonald's Corp. reported that sales at outlets open at least a year increased 8.2 percent in October 2008, while offshore markets and its relatively mature U.S. segment rang up solid gains as well. Systemwide, sales rose 5.4 percent, or 9.9 percent as measured in constant currencies (i.e., an exchange rate that eliminates the effects of exchange rate fluctuations used when calculating financial performance numbers).[17]

How is it that McDonald's still has the energy and drive to run up the hill when Starbucks can barely crawl? The essential reason may be that Starbucks has done nothing nor offered anything different with its product offerings during these difficult economic times. McDonald's, on the other hand, has an entire new line of special offerings that are a combination of lower prices and smaller quantities—all with entirely new branding promoting new customer value, just when the consumers need it the most.

Adding to Starbucks' woes, the ubiquitous burger chain is about to launch a direct attack of its own. In 2009, McDonald's plans to add Starbucks-style premium coffee bars to nearly 14,000 of its U.S.-based restaurants—the biggest diversification ever attempted by the company. McDonald's has already made smaller forays into the coffee market, and with some success. Last year *Consumer Reports* rated its filter coffee (versus espresso coffee) more highly than that offered by Starbucks.[18]

As 3Q08 profits were down by some 97 percent, Starbucks may start desperately discounting its line of premium coffee products.[19] With its business lagging, the company is already fighting back with an "if you can't beat 'em, join 'em" strategy, by offering heated breakfast sandwiches and adding drive-through windows at some store locations.[20] The problem here is that if companies do turn to a "quick fix" rather than looking further down the road and adding value, they will almost certainly fail. Rather, by creating a new branded line of coffee drinks at lower prices and possibly in smaller sizes, Starbucks will acknowledge that times are tough and that it cares about its patrons. At the same time, the company would be preserving brand equity in its perennially successful lineup of premium coffee drinks. A Starbucks Venti Latte, a Grande Mocha Frappuccino, as well as all Starbucks premium coffee drinks should never be discounted—during good or bad times—no matter what.

Discounting takes a toll on profits. At just a 10 percent discount, a typical firm would need to sell 50 percent more units to keep the same profit on the bottom line. Costs also increase in the "discount" game, so companies can literally discount themselves out of business. Instead of cutting cash out of the deal, ask yourself if there is a way you can add value to your product or service. This "value added" proposition means you can "give away" something that won't come out of your profits. Done right, it can also add to the customer experience of both the transaction and your company. A great experience is key to getting that customer's repeat business—which in turn is key to a highly profitable company over time.[21]

Decoupling from Customers by Reducing Sales-Related Expenses

When turbulence is so highly volatile, management that isn't constantly reevaluating the cost and profitability of its transactional customers will find that it will lose money and, eventually, market share.

Studies have shown that only 2 percent to 4 percent of the population is currently in the market to buy any given product or service. That leaves 96 percent to 98 percent who won't buy today, but will be in the market to buy eventually.[22]

When times are tight, it is natural to cater to the here-and-now transactional customers who are ready to buy today. But remember, transactional customers looking for the best deal will come to you for your low price; they will also leave you—and do so quickly—for someone else who has an even lower price.

Management that forgoes investing in the relational consumer, the one who is looking for the trusted brand or expertise and will come back regardless of price, will sooner or later place its company's future in peril. This is especially dangerous when we consider the well-documented research that has uncovered many markets where a small percentage of customers account for a high percentage of total sales. For example, the man who drinks eight Cokes a day is worth much more in profits and attention than the woman who drinks eight Cokes a month.

Studies have shown that unprofitable and highly transactional customer relationships should be reassessed during a recession. When East Asia suffered from a currency crisis in 1997, Singapore Airlines remained profitable by cutting back on short-haul routes and investing $300 million to cater to business and first-class travelers.[23] Singapore Airlines gained the competitive edge by investing in its "high end" travelers, but even though the company cut back on short-haul routes, it didn't cut them out altogether. Moreover, just because the economy may be slow, management cannot neglect the threat of new entrants to its industry or the possibility of product substitutes luring away customers.

Cutting Back on Training and Development Expenses in Economic Crises

When management is trying to weather the storm, investing in training and development is a low priority. Training and development are perceived as expendable costs. But cutting back on this key growth aspect could also cut your share of an already-shrinking market. Can you really afford to lose market share?

Training just doesn't simply affect the bottom line. It gives businesses an opportunity to identify weaknesses or areas where a company needs to improve before the chinks in the armor become apparent to competitors and threaten growth. Conversely, training and development allow a company to keep employees on the cutting edge.

In Australia, for example, a national training evaluation initiative was launched to help make companies from various industries aware of "the significant increase in their bottom line that could occur if they were to identify and pursue the highly profitable training opportunities that often exist within their own enterprises." Training evaluation case studies were carried out on Australian companies ranging in size from 400 to 27,000 employees. The final report revealed positive returns on investment in all cases, with improvements ranging from 30 percent (fuel efficiency training) to 1,277 percent (safety training).[24]

Companies that don't understand the value of training and development will ultimately lose stakeholder value. They may also lose their talent to competitors that are willing to invest in training and development.

Undervaluing Suppliers and Distributors

Suppliers and distributors are the lifeline to a company's ability to put innovation into action. Management that doesn't realize the value of its suppliers and distributors could actually be costing the company money. Suppliers and distributors can help lower near-term costs and give a company sturdy footing when turbulence hits. Chaos seeks to undermine this relationship.

The typical mistakes many companies make regarding their suppliers and distributors *before* turbulence hits are the same ones that many make as knee-jerk reactions *during* turbulent times as a way to preserve cash flow and right the ship. Regrettably, during turbulent times, and especially during tremendously turbulent times, companies need their best suppliers and distributors fully on board with them—fully integrated into company operations.

Turbulent times are particularly revealing times, as well as potentially dangerous ones, according to business negotiations expert Stephen Kozicki, managing partner of Gordian Business Pty. in Sydney, Australia. Kozicki, who helps companies in negotiations with their suppliers, states:

> Managing and negotiating relationships with *all* stakeholders becomes increasingly important during turbulent times. Most companies fail to understand the importance of negotiating with the long term in mind as they prepare to sit down with key suppliers during difficult economic times. Instead, most just default to taking a "big stick" approach to their suppliers and pressuring them to cut their prices. During turbulent times, key suppliers can help companies by coming up with a better product mix, new product and process innovations to solve more problems and reduce costs, or even just helping them with better payment terms through the rough times—some of the most important help any company can get is from a supplier.[25]

An integrated, holistic understanding of *all* stakeholders is crucial to the success of a company in times of change, even chaotic change. Gaining such an understanding will help you make the right choices. If your company doesn't already have its best and highest-quality suppliers and distributors sufficiently integrated, it may be an opportune time to take your relationships with the right suppliers and distributors to the next level. Yet regrettably, too few companies do this. Figure 2–2 lists the ten most common mistakes companies make relative to valued stakeholders during turbulence. Each mistake is followed by the best practices that should be employed.

MISTAKE	BEST PRACTICE
1. Duplication of Capabilities	Best practice suggests that companies should make great efforts to avoid duplication of capabilities between their suppliers and distributors and themselves with a focus on driving out redundancy and costs.
2. Complexity of Contracts	Best practice suggests that companies should have simple contracts based on trust that has been built over the years, including contract execution based upon work with their suppliers and distributors on a day-to-day basis emphasizing continuous improvement and equitably shared cost savings for mutual gains.
3. Insufficient Performance Rating Systems	Best practice suggests that companies should make great efforts to have supplier and distributor rating systems that are easy to understand and give immediate feedback, with special focus on: (1) identifying problem areas, and (2) developing methods to eliminate or mitigate any difficulties, but not used as a tool for penalizing weak performance.
4. Inadequate Product Development/Specification	Best practice suggests that companies should have suppliers and distributors proactively suggest modifications that would improve products and reduce costs, and be rewarded for their effort.
5. Single Dimensional Selection Process	Best practice suggests that rather than having suppliers selected solely by purchasing departments and distributors selected solely by sales departments, companies make their selection based on substantial input from cross-functional teams within the company. This approach moves the company away from the single dimensional criterion for selecting suppliers (low cost) and for selecting distributors (high margin) and toward a strategy to extract full value from supplier and distributor capabilities.
6. Maintaining Physical Separation from Key Suppliers and Distributors	Best practice suggests that the co-location of facilities promotes superior communication between key suppliers and distributors and the company, and further leverages knowledge of all to benefit the company and provides the company greater control over its interests within supplier and distributor operations.

7. Maintaining Too Many Suppliers	Best practice suggests that to improve their supply management, companies are embracing more single-sourcing or reduced sourcing relationships, thereby consolidating their supplier base so that limited resources can be focused on a manageable number of suppliers for them to receive the attention they need to achieve top performance. Similarly, suppliers receive enough volume from the company to warrant investing their own internal resources to optimize their production process and thus produce a component at a more competitive price.
8. Maintaining the Wrong Suppliers and Distributors	Best practice suggests that companies wait too long to eliminate relationships with suppliers and distributors who are poor or marginal performers, or whose relationships with the company are irreparable. During times of turbulence, relationship problems are exacerbated.
9. Failing to Invest in Training for Suppliers and Distributors	Best practice suggests that companies training their suppliers and distributors reduce operating costs and increase sales more than those who do not, and raise the quality of both product and services offered to the company and to its customers.
10. Failing to Invest in Communications with Suppliers and Distributors	Best practice suggests that companies invest in and use various methods to improve communications with their suppliers and distributors and reduce miscommunications and provide feedback on issues of mutual interest, which is especially critical during times of turbulence and disruption in the marketplace. Many companies ask suppliers and distributors to rate them to compare their management practices with those of their direct competitors.

Figure 2–2. Ten most common mistakes made by companies with their stakeholders during turbulence.

Squeezing suppliers is another short-term fix that can do more harm than good. Downturns and turbulence don't last forever. Forcing price cuts from suppliers or coercing distributors to take on more product inventory that the company knows they cannot sell in the next quarter (i.e., "loading the trade") will be remembered long after the turbulence subsides. Costs must be managed carefully. The key is consistency. A company shouldn't act one way in good times and another way in bad times. Otherwise, suppliers, distributors, and other stakeholders in the company's business will lose confidence in the company, and cooperation and productivity will all decline.

When a company doesn't understand the value-added ability to move new products that suppliers and distributors bring to the table, the company will not only fall behind the rest but will be trampled when the storm ends and the sun comes out.

Bank of America seemed to be basking in the sun when on September 15, 2008, it sopped up a failing Merrill Lynch which was about to suffer the same unfortunate fate as Lehman Brothers. BOA had a strong desire to get hold of Merrill Lynch's long-established and profitable private banking and investment banking divisions, including in Europe and Asia. However, shortly after the acquisition, the thunderclouds appeared when Merrill Lynch's losses began to surface. Under heavy pressure from the U.S. Federal Reserve, Bank of America rushed the deal through without adequate due diligence. As a result, in just four short months, between mid-September 2008 and mid-January 2009, Bank of America's market cap dropped to $40 billion from a previous high of $50 billion before its acquisition of Merrill Lynch.

On the brighter side and staying closer to its retail banking roots, Bank of America's track record for creating innovative retail banking services is impressive. For example, it created a rather inventive and commonsense savings account for retail customers. By understanding customer behavior, the bank was able to create a value proposition for its customers. Bank of America realized that most people rounded-up to the next dollar amount when they balanced their checkbooks or wrote checks. For example, if they purchased something for $199.28, they rounded the amount up in their heads and their checkbooks to $200, or if they purchased another item for

$14.95, they'd round up their checkbook entry to $15.00. Bank of America banked on this habit and introduced a service where it would also round up for customers to the next dollar amount on their checking account statements, with the bank putting the rounded difference into a separate interest-bearing savings account for the customer. At the end of the year, these customers had extra cash that was certainly theirs, but which they had not factored into their checkbooks during the previous year.

Most companies can't even see that Bank of America followed people's behaviors, not their rational thinking. People like the idea of having a surprise at the end of the year or when they need some extra cash.

Conclusion

Turbulence and chaos produce the good, the bad, and the ugly. Management's wrong decisions contribute to and amplify the resulting consequences and effects. Management that resorts to financial engineering rather than working on the core fundamentals will compound the precarious footing that chaos creates.

To wit, a former vice president of a leading metals company explained his company's posture in the late 1980s: "The rest of the industry was living in an up cycle, putting their feet up and relaxing. But we were moving to another level to be ready for the next downturn."

In contrast, Citibank was in a precarious situation in 1990 because it had pursued market share growth at the expense of cash flow and profitability. In the words of one senior executive, "You're looking to grow, so you lend aggressively. Credit control wasn't as good as it should have been, and we were emphasizing market share." To keep Citibank from teetering over the edge, the federal regulators stepped in for the next several years to supervise the company's return to financial health.[26]

And look where Citibank is again today—the poster child for the result of bad decisions. Consider that Citigroup is one of the nation's largest issuers of credit cards, with 54 million active accounts. In addition to announcing 50,000 job cuts in mid-November 2008, its credit cards unit had a loss of $902 million in the third quarter of 2008, compared with $1.4 billion in profit a year earlier, as a growing number of customers fell behind or defaulted on their payments. And again, by the end of November 2008, Citigroup asked the U.S. government for an infusion of $20 billion in new capital *and* additional help in shouldering potential losses on $306 billion of high-risk assets.[27]

When management makes wrong decisions during these uncertain times, there is more than just a simple dollar figure involved. Dismissing the creation of value in turbulent times will not only sink the boat, it will take the crew and passengers down with it, as was the case with Citibank. Poor decisions and lack of sound judgment can have a spiraling effect that will leave a company dog-paddling to shore or, worse yet, caught in the untenable riptide. Thriving in a turbulent economy takes more than just luck or gut intuition. It takes a new mindset, serious planning, and the right strategies.

CHAPTER THREE

The *Chaotics* Model

Managing Vulnerability and Opportunity

Giving up the illusion that you can predict the future is a very liberating moment. All you can do is to give yourself the capacity to respond to the only certainty in life—which is uncertainty. The creation of that capability is the purpose of strategy.
—Lord John Browne, Group Chief Executive of BP[1]

IN TIMES OF chaos, the traditional three-year strategic plan is anachronistic and worthless. In fact, the traditional approach to strategy requires precise predictions, which often leads executives to underestimate uncertainty and chaos caused by unpredictable and recurring turbulence. In The Age of Turbulence, this approach can be downright dangerous.

At the core of the traditional approach to strategy lies the assumption that by applying a set of powerful analytical tools, executives can predict the future of any business accurately enough to choose a clear strategic direction for it. When the future is truly turbulent and rises to high levels of chaos, this approach is at best marginally helpful and at worst downright dangerous. Underestimating chaos can lead to strategies that neither defend a company against its vulnerabilities resulting from chaos nor allow it to take advantage of the opportunities arising from chaos.

There is still another danger that lies at the other extreme. If executives can't find a strategy that works for them under traditional analyses, they may decide to abandon the disciplined approach to planning altogether and instead base their decisions on intuition and gut instinct.

As we enter this new era, turbulence will rise and chaos will impact businesses and organizations around the world. Going forward, the new age—The Age of Turbulence—will be characterized by times of a newly defined "normality" punctuated by spurts of prosperity and of downturn (see Figure 3–1). In past years, normality meant largely steady gradual rises and falls that resembled a bird gliding through the sky, sometimes going higher and sometimes swooping lower, but always graceful and in control. In The Age of Turbulence, however, there will be more abrupt and erratic shifts in these smooth trajectories.

And during times of normality, the natural forces of the many new triggers of turbulence begin to accumulate: technological advances and the continuing information revolution; disruptive technologies and innovations; the growing and unsettling effects from rising developing markets elbowing their way into the new echelons perennially belonging only to the mature market elites; hypercompetition from increasingly aggressive competitors who make up the rules as they go along, striking from anywhere and everywhere—and at any time, the forward pushes from sovereign wealth funds and the push-backs from those resisting them; the increasing numbers of vocal business stakeholders; and, finally, the newfound powers that customers and other stakeholders have to create disturbances for businesses whose actions don't resonate well with these new power brokers.

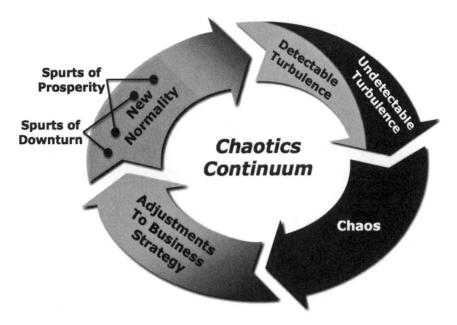

Figure 3–1. Chaotics continuum.

When these triggers accumulate and reach to higher and higher levels, they will erupt into the winds and waves of turbulence. Turbulence can arise at any time, in any form and anywhere—creating varying degrees of disruption and chaos for businesses. It will be the most alert companies, those having early-warning systems already in place, that will detect turbulence. Some turbulence will go completely undetected or will be detected only after the chaos has begun—even by the most vigilant businesses with the most advanced detection systems. Yes, this means that at any time or in any place turbulence can arise suddenly and swiftly, creating chaos and disrupting businesses in ways that top management could not see. And as company executives imagine the worst, many of them will also realize that they cannot do much to protect their companies, even from some of the turbulence that was detected. So, in the end, the best way for them to protect their businesses is to prepare themselves and their organizations as much as they can, to keep their level of paranoia high and remain on high alert.

Such turbulence may occur at the macro level (globally, regionally, or within one country) or at the micro level (within one industry or one company). Predicting turbulence is not possible, so identifying the signs as early as possible becomes one of the critical factors to business success in the future.

Before the 2008 financial meltdown, Citigroup should have heeded the early warnings that were emerging. Meredith Whitman, a bank analyst, declared more than a year earlier: "Citigroup had so mismanaged its affairs that it would need to slash its dividend or go bust." Early on, hedge fund investor Steve Eisman talked about the risks of subprime mortgages. Long Beach Financial "was moving money out the door as fast as it could, few questions asked, in loans built to self-destruct. It specialized in asking homeowners with bad credit and no proof of income to put no money down and defer interest payments for as long as possible. In Bakersfield, California, a Mexican strawberry picker with an income of $14,000 and no English was lent every penny he needed to buy a house for $720,000."[2]

Ivy Zelman, at the time the housing-market analyst at Credit Suisse, had also seen the bubble forming very early on. There's a simple measure of sanity in housing prices: the ratio of median home price to income. Historically, it runs around 3 to 1; by late 2004, it had risen nationally to 4 to 1. "All these people were saying it was nearly as high in some other countries," Zelman says. "But the problem wasn't just that it was 4 to 1. In Los Angeles, it was 10 to 1, and in Miami, 8.5 to 1. And then you coupled that with the buyers. They weren't real buyers. They were speculators."

Once these warnings are ignored, turbulence and chaos erupt, exposing clear vulnerabilities to the business enterprise and causing it to adjust its strategies—and possibly its business model—to overcome any harmful effects. Eisman sensed it and despite the repeated denials by virtually all of the Wall Street "establishment," including the Federal Reserve and the SEC, Eisman shorted his subprime-backed securities, and in doing so he minimized his vulnerability and exploited opportunities the experts missed.

Suppose in a live interview on CNBC today, your biggest competitor's president makes a new product announcement with new industry-shattering breakthrough technology that the industry has

Global credit and capital markets reopen and recover

Severe global recession ← → **Moderate global recession**

Scenario: Battered but resilient
- Prolonged recession of 18 months or more
- New, effective regulatory regime
- Recovery generated by effective fiscal, monetary policies and led by selected geographies (e.g., China, Middle East, United States)
- Safe leverage ratios reached, leading to slow resumption of trading and lending volume
- Moderate recovery of trade and capital flows
- Globalization gradually gets back on course
- Attitudes slowly rebound

Scenario: Regenerated global momentum
- Moderate recession of 2 to 4 quarters, followed by strong economic growth
- New, effective regulatory regime
- Safe leverage ratios reached, leading to rapid expansion of trading and lending volumes
- Cost of capital recovers to historic levels
- Trade and capital flows recover quickly
- Globalization stays on course; developed and emerging economies remain linked
- Attitudes rebound, become positive

Scenario: Long freeze
- Recession lasts for more than 5 years, as in Japan during the 1990s
- Ineffective regulatory, fiscal, and monetary policies
- All geographies stagnate
- Defensive leverage ratios, with restricted credit flows and trading in illiquid markets
- Significant government involvement in allocation of credit
- Very slow recovery of trade and capital flows
- Globalization goes into reverse
- Attitudes become much more defensive and nationalistic

Scenario: Stalled globalization
- Moderate recession of 1 to 2 years, followed by slow economic growth
- Regulatory regime holds system together, but with significant drag on economy (e.g., higher cost of intermediation)
- Overly safe leverage ratios
- Significant government involvement in allocation of credit
- Significantly higher cost of capital than before crisis
- Globalization stalls
- Attitudes become more defensive and nationalistic

Global credit and capital markets close down and remain volatile

Figure 3–2. Four economic scenarios and possible outcomes. *(Source: "Hard, Harder, Hardest Times," from "Leading Through Uncertainty," by Lowell Bryan and Diana Farrell, The McKinsey Quarterly, December 2008.)*

been dreaming about for the last five years that all but makes obsolete your most profitable and biggest product line. The question is: How did you miss seeing how close your company's biggest competitor—or any competitor, for that matter—was to reaching such game-changing success in your industry?

Turbulence may alternatively open up new opportunities for your business that can be exploited with your present business model or with a revised model. Suddenly you get an urgent call from your CFO who is attending a credit-swap and derivative symposium in Chicago. He is calling to inform you that he just learned that your biggest competitor is planning to file for bankruptcy protection later that day. The competitor's main plant burned down and the competitor lacked insurance coverage. Bankers are demanding the competitor repay pending defaulting senior debt. Your CFO tells you that the competitor's CEO is holding for you on the other telephone line, prepared to offer you the deal of a lifetime. And you never saw it coming.

Chaotic situations like this one will occur time and again, creating opportunities and/or crises. Organizations will have to learn how to seize the extraordinary opportunities that arise during periods of immense uncertainty. Business leaders must now begin to evaluate a broad set of macroeconomic outcomes, construct an equally broad set of scenarios with appropriate strategic responses, and then take actions to make their companies more responsive, robust, and resilient.

A December 2008 *McKinsey Quarterly* article spoke to the uncertainty surrounding the global credit crisis and the global recession. The McKinsey article described the wide range of possible outcomes in four scenarios shown in Figure 3–2 and further noted that many permutations were possible.[3]

Each company will need to insert additional industry and company trends and events to enrich the scenarios. Business executives will need to create strategic and tactical options for defense and offense for the more likely scenarios—and do so quickly.

The ultimate goal of all business leaders is to create a viable, vibrant, growing, and profitable company that can sustain itself for the benefit of all of its stakeholders—and do so for as long as possible. As you and your organizations progress through the work of *Chaotics,* the goal is to attain a high level of Business Enterprise Sustainability for your company. To do so, your company will need to exploit the opportunities created by chaos—and seen at the *chaos inflection points*—and take the necessary protective measures to minimize any potential damage by your company's exposed vulnerabilities (see Figure 3–3). We will explore Business Enterprise Sustainability (BES) in Chapter 6.

As we discussed in Chapter 1, Andy Grove's *strategic inflection points*[4] occur in all businesses as a direct result of specific forces affecting particular businesses. Often they render your business strategy obsolete and demand a new game-changing strategy. A well-publicized strategic inflection point came for two venerable firms on September 21, 2008. On that day Goldman Sachs and Morgan Stanley, the last two independent U.S. investment banks, became bank holding companies, a move that fundamentally altered the

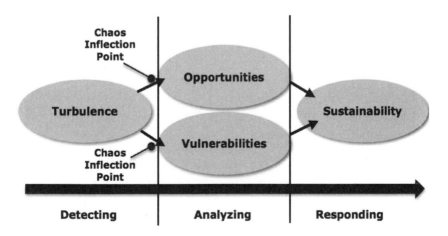

Figure 3–3. From turbulence to sustainability.

landscape of Wall Street by signaling the demise of the Glass-Steagall Act, the epochal legislation of 1933 that split investment banks and retail banks after the start of the Great Depression.[5]

Turbulence is erratic—and it's unpredictable. It triggers certain levels of chaos, which punctuates the new normality as shown in Figure 3–4.

A company's failure to successfully navigate its way through a strategic inflection point causes business to decline. One of the clearest examples of a company's—or maybe even an entire industry's—failure to successfully navigate its way through a strategic inflection point is the current situation of the Big Three U.S. automakers—GM, Ford, and Chrysler—whose individual and collective strategic inflection points have long passed, with none of them transforming into new business models, but scrambling just to stay alive. All of these automakers are in the business of creating transportation vehicles for moving passengers and for shipping

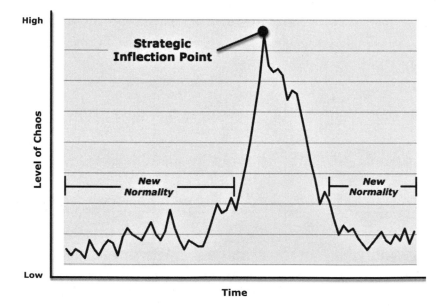

Figure 3–4. Chaos punctuated new normality.

cargo—*today and tomorrow.* This point has been very clear for many decades. The Big Three are not in the sole business of creating or developing—or perpetuating—internal combustion engines based on petroleum-based energy fuels. Long before the spike of oil prices that topped $150.00 a barrel in July 2008, the handwriting was on the wall: They needed to make some dramatic changes in their technologies, and certainly in their very business models. Minimally, if they couldn't see it for themselves, they could have at least begun to take notice of foreign automakers' forays into hybrids and alternative energy vehicles several years earlier. After all, these were the very same foreign automakers that toppled the decades-long market dominance of the Big Three. The U.S. auto industry had multiple strategic inflection points, long before their CEOs found themselves sitting before the U.S. Congress in November 2008 with their hands out, pleading for money to keep their failed companies afloat. Each time, they failed to recognize that their business models were continuing to decline further and further.

Once the strategic inflection point is reached, business leaders are forced to deal with their companies' previously unexposed vulnerabilities, or their newly revealed opportunities—and do so with deliberate and sometimes bold action that oftentimes requires developing a new mindset, which is needed to push past now-obsolete strategies and business models. Typically, a new mindset means getting upfront and close to the sources of the changes that may be at the core of unexposed vulnerabilities. Here's just a short list of new behaviors that should be considered:[6]

1. *Business leaders and top executives must begin to see change first-hand.* They should visit places where change is happening. They need to feel the change personally, not just read about it in a business magazine, learn about it from a consultant, or get it in a report from an employee. Instead, they need to visit a nanotech or biotech lab, talk with a group of twenty-year-olds to understand how they think, hold discussions with ardent environmentalists or antiglobalization activists. As the rate of change increases, so must the personal commitment by senior executives to understand it.

2. *Executive management must eliminate the filters.* Business leaders must make sure their views are not censored, and their access to unpleasant truths not blocked by anyone in their organizations who may be motivated to protect them. Talk to potential customers who aren't buying from your company. Go out to dinner with your most freethinking employees. Establish a shadow executive committee whose members are, on average, ten to twenty years younger than the "real" executive committee. Review the proposals that never got past division heads or VPs. Tell everyone in the company that the CEO's office accepts e-mail, open and anonymous, from employees proposing new ideas for making money or saving money.

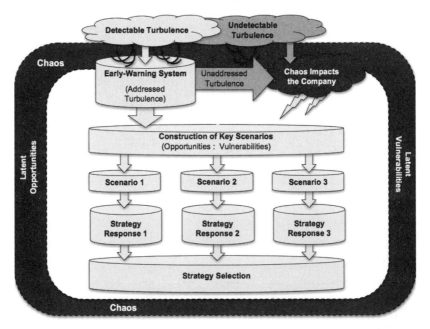

Figure 3–5. Chaotics management system.

3. *Business leaders must accept the inevitability of strategy decay.* While it is easy to admit that nothing lasts forever, it is more difficult for top executives to admit that one of their strategies is beginning to lose steam.

Beyond developing a new mindset, business executives must drop their reliance on a two-playbook strategy—one for up-markets and the other for down-markets—and continuously fine-tune their strategies or even discard them when the environment demands it. The primary difficulty lies in the fact that their strategies begin to settle down, get optimized, and become entrenched more deeply during stretches of normality, which leaves them unprepared when turbulence breaks out.

What follows is a framework for such a new system—the *Chaotics Management System* (see Figure 3–5).

Chaotics management is a systematic approach to detecting, analyzing, and responding to turbulence and its chaos. The chaotics management system consists of the following three components:

- Detecting sources of turbulence through development of *Early-Warning Systems*

- Responding to chaos by the *Construction of Key Scenarios*

- *Selecting Strategy* based on scenario prioritization and risk attitude

Constructing an Early-Warning System (EWS)

We know that turbulence may come at any time or from any place, and that some of it will be detectable and some of it will not. Turbulence that is detected should be analyzed and then acted on as quickly as possible to be able to identify (1) the opportunities that may be revealed and exploited and (2) the vulnerabilities to the business so they can be minimized or negated altogether.

Turbulence that goes undetected, including turbulence that is detected but that management is unable or unwilling to act on, or act on quickly enough, will create chaos for the company. For example, recall the number of times when you've been flying on a business trip and the pilot comes on the public address system before your flight takes off or after you are already in the air to announce that there has been reported severe turbulence in your flight path to your destination city. Traffic control, the pilot says, has rerouted your flight to avoid the turbulence, which will cause your arrival to be delayed by thirty minutes. Without having sophisticated weather radar and detections systems in place that constantly convey vital information to air traffic control, and having constant communications from those flights that got hammered by unexpected and unpredicted turbulence, your flight could be a very rough one.

Now imagine that your flight has already taken off and that after an hour your plane hits an unexpected air pocket or runs into an unforeseen downdraft that neither your pilots nor air traffic control had any inkling of. The plane and all the passengers and crew are rocked back and forth violently until your pilots can react and chart a new flight plan and get everyone out of harm's way.

Now, finally, imagine that on that same flight, as you are waiting to be served your drinks and dinner after a long and tough day, the pilot gets on the PA system to announce that there is severe turbulence just ahead, and it's so massive that there is no way to avoid it. The pilot tells all of you that for your own safety dinner and drinks will not be served until the flight is safely through the turbulence. Then everyone waits nervously for the rough ride to begin.

Just as a jumbo jet's pilot and crew prepares for each of its flights, so too must business executives and their organizations prepare steps to move their business strategies forward and execute them during turbulent times. The first step is to develop an effective early warning

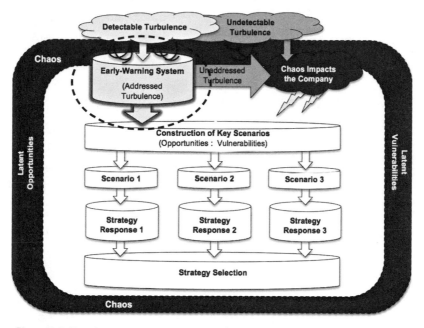

Figure 3–6. *Chaotics management system: early-warning system.*

system that will detect as much turbulence as possible, as quickly as possible and as far in advance as possible (see Figure 3–6).

As business executives begin to consider developing an effective early warning system in their companies, they need to be very clear about the goals. In addition to issuing warnings and alerts, goals should include identifying and reducing risk, uncertainty, and vulnerability, as well as recognizing and exploiting opportunities. Raising awareness and educating people in their organizations are important goals. Often, advance warnings are actually observed by many within an organization who just don't realize the importance of what they see.

Two respected thought leaders in the development of business early-warning systems are George S. Day and Paul J. H. Schoemaker of the Wharton School's Mack Center for Technological Innovation. In their book, *Peripheral Vision: Detecting the Weak Signals That Will Make or Break Your Company,* they state that "the biggest dangers to a company are the ones you don't see coming, and understanding these threats—and anticipating opportunities—requires strong peripheral vision."[7]

For example, Day and Schoemaker cite Mattel, the perennial leader in children's toys and dolls, which lost 20 percent of its share of the worldwide fashion-doll segment between 2001 and 2004 to smaller rivals including MGA Entertainment, which created a new line of dolls called Bratz. MGA recognized what Mattel didn't—that preteen girls were becoming more sophisticated and maturing more quickly. They were outgrowing Barbie earlier than ever before and preferred dolls that looked more like their teenage siblings and the pop stars they idolized. As the target market for Barbie narrowed from girls ages 3 to 11 to girls ages 3 to 5, the Bratz line cut Barbie's market share rapidly and deeply. By the time Mattel finally moved to rescue Barbie's declining fortunes with a new line of hipper fashion dolls, the damage was done and Barbie, queen of dolls for more than forty years, had lost a fifth of her realm almost overnight—and Mattel didn't see it coming.[8] (Mattel, meanwhile, was also pursuing a lawsuit against MGA, claiming that a former Mattel designer who subsequently went to work for MGA and created MGA's Bratz line had, in fact, created the original Bratz concept while earlier employed by Mattel. In December 2008, Mattel won a judgment against MGA to revert the Bratz line back to Mattel and for MGA to cease its production of the Bratz line.)

Day and Schoemaker make the further point that "when a company examines its main areas of focus, its questions are targeted and the answers precise: What is our market share? What are our profits? Have our sales volumes increased? What is our employee turnover? What are our competitors up to? But the questions used to examine the periphery need to be much more open-ended and the answers far less precise. For example, as part of Johnson & Johnson's strategy process, the organization's executive committee and members of a strategy task force asked themselves: What will the demographics of 2010 look like? What will a typical doctor's office look like? What role will governments play? What role will payers play?"[9]

Often, when business leaders begin to contemplate developing a formal early warning system in their companies, one of the first things they will examine are the important pieces of information and market intelligence that they and their organizations missed in the past, and which created the biggest surprises for them. The fact is, most surprises do not occur for lack of early signs, but for lack of a culture and mindset open to seeing them. The key areas to be watched are customers and channels; competitors and complementors; emerging technologies and scientific developments (disruptive innovations and technologies); political, legal, social, and economic forces; and influencers and shapers.

Day and Schoemaker recommend that business leaders begin by answering eight key questions, and then create ongoing discussions around these questions at the opening round of meetings to kick off any early-warning systems development:[10]

1. What have been our past blind spots? What is happening in these past blind spots now?

2. Is there an instructive analogy from another industry?

3. What important signals are we rationalizing away?

4. Who in our industry is skilled at picking up weak signals and acting on them ahead of everyone else?

5. What are our mavericks and outliers trying to tell us?

6. What future surprises could really hurt (or help) us?

7. What emerging technologies could change the game?

8. Is there an unthinkable scenario?

Another expert working in the area of early-warning systems, Ben Gilad, presses the same recurring theme—namely, businesses just don't see what is in front of them. Gilad's focus is on the external environment so that companies can avoid being blindsided by the unexpected. Gilad's is a focused, three-part competitive early-warning system designed to avoid what he calls "industry dissonance," which occurs when market realities have outpaced a company's strategy. Gilad's system involves three distinct yet interdependent components:[11]

- *Risk Identification.* What are the potential market and industry developments to which a company would be vulnerable?

- *Risk Monitoring.* What movement exists from competitors or in the business landscape that might indicate these factors are (or will soon be) in play?

- *Management Action.* Are executives kept aware of risk dynamics, and are they equipped to launch a swift and aggressive response before their organization is harmed?

"Good facts, and lots of them, lead to good decisions," says Russell Chapman, a partner at Acclaro Partners in Reston, Virginia, a strategy consulting firm that provides advisory services to middle-market companies. "We have been extraordinarily successful helping our clients survive and thrive during even the most challenging times by getting them to accept an important but difficult lesson: Neither fact-based decision making nor changing strategic direction when conditions warrant is a sign of weakness at the top. We are always fascinated by how enthusiastically CEOs embrace a structured decision-making process when they realize it takes the pressure off them to always be right."

Let's return to Detroit's Big Three automakers—GM, Ford, and Chrysler—and consider what even a minimal early-warning system might have told them. Even before they were lobbying the U.S. Congress in late 2008 for a $25 billion bailout of the industry, it was apparent that the Big Three's major problems began a long time before the global financial crises and the recessions hit the United States, Europe, and most of the rest of the world in late 2008. One would have imagined that one or all of the Big Three automakers would have engaged in a bit of chaotics management long before the day they were called before the U.S. Congress. But they didn't, nor could they present even an outline of a viable business model to lead their companies to success when asked pointedly by Congressional members who pressed the executives on how they would spend U.S. taxpayers' monies if given to them. The perverse irony of the situation is that on the very same day, Honda was opening a new automobile production facility in Indiana, employing more than 1,000 new workers. In the first nine months of 2008, Honda registered a rise in U.S. sales to a record 11 percent market share, making it the world's fourth largest automaker, behind Toyota, GM, and Ford.[12]

Let's imagine how the Big Three might have answered the eight key questions as far back as five years before their bailout request:

1. *What have been our past blind spots? What is happening in these past blind spots now?* Answer: Steady growth of foreign automakers has eroded the Big Three's U.S. market share, based on U.S. auto buyers' increasing preference for foreign automakers' designs and value. There is also the matter of pension plans becoming a growing percentage of the total operating cost of the business, especially with a rapidly aging workforce.

2. *Is there an instructive analogy from another industry?* Answer: The United States has relinquished U.S. (and world) market share to Asian manufacturers of televisions, audio and video players, PCs,

and other consumer electronics. There is also the example of the U.S. steel manufacturing industry.

3. *What important signals are we rationalizing away?* Answer: Americans (and others outside of the United States) will prefer to buy U.S.-designed and manufactured automobiles and trucks even if they don't meet consumer needs and cannot compete on quality with foreign manufacturers' vehicles; the pension funding problem will be funded by big increases in revenues and profits from Americans preferring to buy more from the Big Three.

4. *Who in our industry is skilled at picking up weak signals and acting on them ahead of everyone else?* Answer: Japanese, Korean, and European automobile and truck manufacturers.

5. *What are our mavericks and outliers trying to tell us?* Answer: Environmental and alternative energy concerns are becoming more important to Americans; the power of the "green movement" is rising in the United States.

6. *What future surprises could really hurt (or help) us?* Answer: The price of a gallon of gasoline in the United States goes above $3.00, prompting U.S. auto and truck buyers to buy smaller and more fuel efficient vehicles; sales and profits do not increase faster than the Big Three's pension liabilities.

7. *What emerging technologies could change the game?* Answer: All alternative energy technologies, and especially the technologies being promoted by Asian automobile manufacturers in new vehicles that will be available in the United States. Honda began to sell an electric hybrid in the United States in 2000.

8. *Is there an unthinkable scenario? What is it?* Answer: Oil goes over $150 a barrel, prompting a gallon of gas to top $5.00, and the United States goes into a deep recession, prompting buyers to stop purchasing autos and trucks.

Yes, one may argue that hindsight is 20/20 and that it is easy to lay blame at the feet of the Big Three for missing these early-warning signals for at least a decade. The simple fact remains that with more focus on seeing the many signs and signals from the marketplace and the economy overall, the Big Three would have fared much better over the past several years and wouldn't have faced the issue of insolvency when *all* of their foreign competitors faced, at worst, a temporary downturn in their businesses during the worst of the economic crises.

Construction of Key Scenarios

In his book *Inevitable Surprises,* Peter Schwartz writes that a few years ago he was contacted by Robert Rubin, the vice chairman of Citicorp and former Secretary of the Treasury under President Bill Clinton. "We keep getting surprised by big things," Rubin stated, as he asked Schwartz to meet with him and Citicorp's advisory board and its top executives. "Tell us what the big surprises are going to be. We want to avoid them," Rubin concluded. As Schwartz goes on to tell the story, when he met with Rubin and his top advisers and executives in the strategic planning meeting, he found that, individually, the executives at Citicorp already knew most of the issues and challenges looming before them. However, no one had put all of them together to make sense of the complete picture of the biggest challenges facing Citicorp in the future. No wonder Citicorp executives kept getting surprised.[13]

Citicorp's top executives were aware of many discrete challenges that could impact their individual businesses, but silos prevented anyone from having the necessary helicopter or balcony view. The biggest problem is that they didn't put all the information together to see the big picture. A core strategic discipline of the chaotics management system is that a business's leaders must draw together the views of top executives from all departments, as well as other subject matter experts and company stakeholders (internal and external), to begin to construct highly probable key scenarios that the company could confront. At the very least, there should be a worst-case scenario, a most-expected scenario, and a best-case scenario. And in times of increased turbulence, business leaders need to push their groups to investigate and analyze more possible situations, including the most feared scenarios.

As shown in Figure 3–7, key scenarios must be constructed along with the strategy responses that would be appropriate for each scenario.

Constructing scenarios is a strategic planning method that organizations use to make flexible long-term plans. It is in large part an adaptation and generalization of classic methods originally used by military intelligence in what has come to be known as "war games." The original method was that a group of analysts would generate simulation games for policymakers. In business applications, the

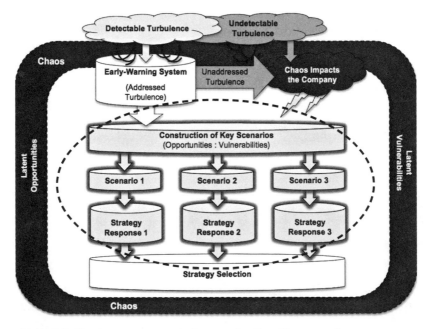

Figure 3–7. Chaotics management system: construction of key scenarios.

emphasis on *gaming* remains, although there are more techniques for scenario planning as well.[14]

Effective scenario construction requires identifying the turbulence drivers in the environment that could create chaos. Trends will capture momentum and continuity, but one must also imagine surprise occurrences. Royal Dutch Shell started its scenario planning system several years ago, after the oil crises of the 1970s had made the company's top executives increasingly aware of the surprises and turbulence lurking in the marketplace.

When business leaders and their executive teams begin constructing multiple scenarios, a lot depends on how much uncertainty exists. A recent McKinsey report distinguished between four levels of uncertainty, each having its own characteristics:[15]

Level 1: *A clear enough future* can be identified in which residual uncertainty is irrelevant to making strategic decisions, so managers can develop a single forecast that is a sufficiently precise basis for their strategies. Here, only one scenario is constructed. To help generate this prediction of the future, managers can use standard strategy tools that include market research, analyses of competitors' costs and capacity, value chain analysis, and Michael Porter's five-forces framework. Discounted cash flow models that incorporate those predictions can then be used to determine the value of alternative strategies.

Level 2: *Alternative futures* are identified, in which the future is described as one of a few discrete scenarios. Analysis cannot identify which outcome will actually occur, but it helps establish probabilities; some or all elements of the key strategy would change if one of the predicted outcomes were realized. Here, managers construct a few scenarios and estimate the probability of each scenario's occurrence. The value of a strategy depends mainly on competitors' strategies, which cannot yet be observed or predicted. For example, in oligopoly markets, such as chemicals and basic raw materials, the primary uncertainty is often competitors' plans for expanding capacity. Economies of scale often dictate that any plant built would be quite large and would be likely to have a significant impact on industry prices and profitability. Therefore, any one company's decision to build a plant is often contingent on competitors' decisions. The company has to calculate the payoffs for four situations: if they built a plant and the competitor did not; if they built a plant and the competitor built one; if the competitor built one and they did not; and finally, if neither of them built a plant. This is a classic level 2 situation: The possible outcomes are discrete and clear, and it is difficult to predict which outcome will occur.

Level 3: *A range of potential futures* can be identified with a limited number of key variables. There are no natural discrete scenarios, and some or all elements of strategy would change with each scenario. Here, managers construct several scenarios because of the great complexity of the underlying factors. Scenarios that describe the extreme points in the range of possible outcomes are often relatively easy to develop, but they rarely provide much concrete guidance for current strategic decisions. Three general rules are used to assist in scenario planning: (1) Develop only a limited number of alternative scenarios—the complexity of juggling more than four or five scenarios tends to hinder decision making; (2) avoid developing redundant scenarios that have no unique implications for strategic decision making; and (3) develop a set of scenarios that collectively account for the probable range of future outcomes and not necessarily the entire possible range.

Level 4: *True ambiguity* exists, in which a number of dimensions of uncertainty interact to create an environment that is virtually impossible to predict. Here, it just isn't possible to create a reasonable number of scenarios to analyze with great precision, so decisions are made intuitively and at the moment. Even if it is impossible to develop a meaningful set of probable or even possible outcomes, managers can gain a valuable strategic perspective. Usually, they can identify at least a subset of the variables determining how the market will evolve over time. They can also identify indicators of these variables. These indicators, some favorable and others unfavorable, will let them track the market's evolution over time and adapt their strategy as new information becomes available. Early detection of market changes and analogies from similar markets will help sort out whether such beliefs are realistic.

In the context of extreme chaos that falls outside the realm of McKinsey's four levels of uncertainty, searching for right answers would be pointless: The relationships between cause and effect are impossible to determine because they shift constantly and no manageable patterns exist—only extreme turbulence and chaos. This is the realm of *unknowables*. The events of September 11, 2001, fall into this category.[16] The immediate job of the business leader is not to discover patterns but to stop the bleeding. A leader must first act to establish order, then sense where stability is present and where it is absent, and then respond by working to transform the situation from chaos to complexity to some order, where the identification of emerging patterns can both help prevent future crises and discern new opportunities. Communication of the most direct top-down or broadcast kind is imperative; there is simply no time to ask for input.

Though the events of September 11 were not immediately comprehensible, the crisis demanded decisive action. Mayor Rudy Giuliani demonstrated exceptional effectiveness under extreme chaotic conditions by issuing directives and taking action to reestablish order. However, in his role as New York City's mayor, he was criticized for the same top-down leadership style that proved so enormously effective during the catastrophe. A specific danger for leaders following a crisis is that some of them become less successful when the context shifts because they are unable to switch styles to match the changed circumstances.[17]

Returning to turbulence that is more detectable, active engagement in scenario construction provides business leaders with the ability to gain deeper insights and have greater flexibility in setting strategies. When approached this way, some groups of facts become more important than others. Consequently, managers can refine their information search, looking for further cues and patterns and testing their ideas and their strategic responses. The principal value of such scenario planning is that it allows business leaders to "rehearse the future," an opportunity that does not present itself in day-to-day operations where every action and decision counts.

Here is one effective and efficient approach to scenario construction:[18]

1. *Decide on the key question to be answered by the scenario analysis.* Then it is possible to assess whether scenario planning is preferred over other methods or analysis by analogy.

2. *Set the scope and time of the analysis.* Take into consideration how quickly changes have happened in the past, and try to assess to what degree it is possible to predict trends in demographics, product life cycles, or other categories of interest.

3. *Identify major stakeholders.* Decide who will be affected and have an interest in the possible outcomes. Identify their current interests and whether and why these interests have changed over time in the past.

4. *Map basic trends and turbulence and the consequent chaotic forces.* This mapping includes industry, competitive,

economic, political, technological, legal, and societal trends. Use brainstorming techniques to assess to what degree these trends affect your research questions; then describe each trend, including how and why it will affect the organization and your business.

5. *Find key uncertainties resulting in chaos.* Include chaotic forces that would have an important impact on the industry, the marketplace, and your business. Assess whether any linkages exist between different chaotic forces, and rule out any "impossible" scenarios.

6. *Define the key scenarios.* Usually two to four scenarios are constructed. Plot them on a grid if possible. One approach is to put all positive elements into one scenario and all negative elements in another, and then refine the remaining scenarios. Avoid pure best-case and worst-case scenarios. Identify and conduct any additional research that may be still needed.

7. *Assess the key scenarios.* Are they relevant for the goal? Are they internally consistent? Are they archetypical? Do they represent relatively stable outcome situations?

8. *Converge toward decision scenarios.* Retrace the previous seven steps in an iterative process until you reach scenarios that address the fundamental issues facing the organization. Assess upsides and downsides of each scenario, and then prioritize each one, based on a probability assessment.

Let's return to our example of the Big Three U.S. automakers and develop a quick outline of one possible scenario construction exercise (see Figure 3–8).

STEP	IMPACT
1. Decide on the key question to be answered by the scenario analysis.	Impact of the increasing cost of pension liabilities.
2. Set the scope and time of the analysis.	U.S.-based employees with company-funded pension plans (2004–2008).
3. Identify major stakeholders.	Employees, labor unions, consumers, auto dealers, suppliers, banks, pension fund companies managing pension funds—all under increased levels of stress to varying degrees.
4. Map basic trends and turbulence, and the consequent chaotic forces.	Rapidly aging employee population with disproportionately lower rate of younger workers entering the autoworker workforce versus rate of retirees; increasing volatility in stock market where pension funds are invested; downward profit margin pressure from foreign competitors with increasing market share and lower prices from lower costs (nonunion U.S. employees); foreign-made imports from low-cost markets; increasing labor rates and health care costs; increasingly combative union positions due to shrinking union membership.
5. Find key uncertainties resulting in chaos.	Rapid surges in the price of gasoline due to volatile oil price rises (and sudden disruptive declines, as was the case in late 2008), shifting consumer demand away from larger and less fuel-efficient vehicles; aggressive expansion by foreign automakers in the U.S. market, putting downward pressure on sales volume and upward pressure on costs; economic slowdown or recession in the U.S.; surges in raw material, supplies, and component parts prices, due to increased global demand, especially from high-growth emerging markets.
6. Define the key scenarios.	Positive Scenario: Substantial increase in U.S. demand pushes volumes up to record levels and substantially increases profit, which will be invested into pension plan funds in the equities market averaging 25 percent year-on-year returns; at the same time the U.S. government passes legislation raising the retirement age for

all Americans covered by company-funded pension plans to age 70, up from 65 years. Negative Scenario: Simultaneous bursting of multiple asset bubbles (real estate, equities, etc.), driving the U.S. into a deep, protracted recession; banking industry stressed by defaulting subprime mortgages, creating a credit-crunch triggering bank failures and prolonged deflation.

7. Assess the key scenarios.	Negative Scenario is more probable than the Positive Scenario by a yet-to-be-determined but substantial probability, based upon current information.
8. Converge toward decision scenarios.	Most probably, scenarios weighted toward Negative Scenario; develop alternative strategies and new business models to preempt or mitigate total financial collapse.

Figure 3–8. Big Three automakers scenario construction exercise (sample).

This procedure for building scenarios is more sophisticated than the normal work of doing "contingency planning." Contingency planning usually imagines one major variable and how the firm might respond if that variable changes. How would our company respond if our competitor cut his price in half, or if he came out with a new machine that performed 20 percent better than ours? But scenarios focus on the joint effect of several factors that more closely resemble the real world confronted by business leaders. Constructing scenario plans therefore helps business leaders understand how the various threads of a complex tapestry move if one or more threads are pulled. When business leaders and their teams explore all of the factors together, they soon realize certain combinations could magnify the impact. This may give even greater insight into their possible futures.[19]

One final note on early-warning systems and why *clear signs*— even very clear signs—are often missed. Paul Krugman, the Nobel and Pulitzer Prize winner and columnist for *The New York Times*, wrote an op–ed piece in the aftermath of the financial meltdown of 2008. "A few months ago I found myself at a meeting of economists and finance officials, discussing—what else?—the crisis," he wrote. "There was a lot of soul-searching going on. One senior policymaker asked, 'Why didn't we see this coming?'" According to Krugman, "One answer to these questions is that nobody likes a party pooper." Krugman went on:

> While the housing bubble was still inflating, lenders were making lots of money issuing mortgages to anyone who walked in the door; investment banks were making even more money repackaging those mortgages into shiny new securities; and money managers who booked big paper profits by buying those securities with borrowed funds looked like geniuses, and were paid accordingly. Who wanted to hear from dismal economists warning that the whole thing was, in effect, a giant Ponzi scheme? There's also another reason the economic policy establishment failed to see the current crisis coming. The crises of the 1990s and the early years of this decade should have been seen as dire omens, as intimations of still worse troubles to come. But everyone was too busy celebrating our success in getting through those crises to notice.[20]

Scenario and Strategy Selection

Following the construction of key scenarios, business leaders need to meet and select the most probable ones. For each scenario, they should work out the most appropriate strategy response. However, this doesn't mean that they are to choose one of these three scenarios and strategies. Rather, they realize they don't know what will happen. They will want to adopt a strategy that satisfies the amount of risk and opportunity they are willing to accept. One executive may argue that they should assume the worst-case scenario and adopt the corresponding strategy that would work if it happens (often called a *mini-max strategy*—minimize the maximum risk). Another executive may say that the scenario featuring a lot of opportunities is the one worth constructing a strategy for because it could make them winners. Still another executive may say that the turbulence is not likely to last and they should return to the strategy that has worked well in the past.

The main point is that there is too much uncertainty to know which scenario will occur. But the exercise of searching for a strategy that would do fairly well against whatever happens is worthwhile. And if something quite different happens, they have already thought through other possible responses (see Figure 3–9).

Let's take a moment to recap where we are. The company will be operating an early-warning system supplying signals as to what might happen to render its current strategy obsolete and warn managers of a strategy inflection point. If they ignore these signals, considerable turbulence and chaos may follow. The company should add to its thinking further unpredictable surprises and capture these possibilities in a limited number of scenarios. Management needs to think through how it would strategically respond to each of the scenario narratives. It doesn't have to choose one scenario (and its accompanying strategy) as the most likely. But it does have to decide how much risk versus opportunity to go after. This process may lead to a blended strategy that everyone agrees will leave the company best off in the face of uncertainty. If management is wrong about what takes place, then it can shift to a more appropriate strategy that goes with the new condition. At least the company has thought through other responses in advance of having to put any of them into practice.

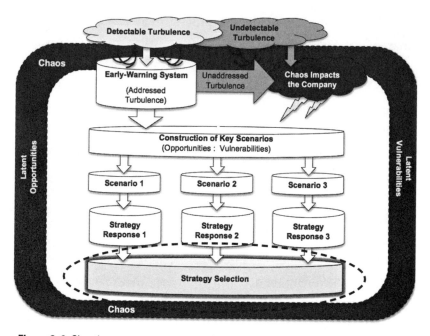

Figure 3–9. *Chaotics management system: key scenario and strategy selection.*

In the meantime, the chaotics management system has exposed the company to some major vulnerabilities as well as opportunities. The company can work on reducing its more critical vulnerabilities while devoting attention to its most salient opportunities. The company has a flexible response system, depending on what eventualities take place.

Companies will also need to establish response systems for each scenario down to each functional department and geographic location. For example, when large fires break out in Southern California, there is an acknowledged set of steps that firefighters and the local governments use to put the fires out as quickly as possible, with as little damage as possible. Similarly, when hurricanes or tsunamis are detected in the Caribbean or Indian Ocean, different islands, individually or together, have a standard set of preparations to warn residents and to get them out of the danger zones ahead of the intense turbulence and the damage it will cause.

Similarly, companies should have similar fast and/or automatic responses. IKEA, Sweden's giant furniture company, has many automatic response systems. For example, when sales of selected expensive items drop either in a single store or in a predefined geographic area or region, IKEA automatically increases the floor space devoted to cheaper furniture items and simultaneously decreases the floor space showing expensive items. Alternatively, IKEA does the reverse when sales of the expensive items get stronger.

The owner of a chain of fifty cinemas in the United States constantly watches attendance numbers for specific movies and quickly moves a movie that has slowed down in attendance in a prime high-volume theater to outlying theaters in lower-volume attendance locations. The rationale is to maximize ticket revenue at both prime cinema locations and outlying cinema locations across the entire fifty-location chain.

In a well-known case illustrating how automatic response strategies can help to support business strategy, the largest low-cost airline in the United States, Southwest Airlines, persevered through the industrywide downturn following September 11, 2001, to remain one of the world's most profitable airlines, posting a profit for the thirty-fifth consecutive year in January 2008.[21] In the 1990s, Southwest Airlines initiated a sophisticated automatic response hedging strategy to reduce its fuel costs by as much as 50 percent. The strategy has generated gains in excess of $4 billion, including $1 billion in 2005 alone—105 percent of Southwest's operating income for that year. Less often discussed is the reasoning behind Southwest's automatic response to making hedging decisions. For Southwest's executives, hedging fuel-cost risk was only part of a larger strategy centered on the stability of costs, service levels, and fares. They knew that rising fuel prices were the biggest threat to their business model, and they chose to remain a low-cost carrier no matter what happened. If fuel prices rose, their hedge meant they would win in the market because their labor and productivity advantages would be strengthened by an edge in fuel prices as well. If prices stayed flat or fell, they would still be the low-cost leader. As a result, Southwest profited by being the first airline to recognize that oil-price risk need not be a natural risk for an airline to bear.[22]

Conclusion

Today and into the future, it may not be as critical to ask what businesses own and produce as it is to ask about their ability to detect turbulence, anticipate chaos, and manage risk. Identifying and managing risk is far from straightforward. Constructing scenarios and strategies to deal with anticipated risks, and conversely, exploiting opportunities, requires business leaders to instill new strategic behaviors and disciplines in the organization.

And when these new and necessary behaviors are instilled in the daily decision-making processes, it creates a momentum and a culture that systematically overcomes turbulence's chaos and routinely beats the competition. Such companies will succeed in The Age of Turbulence, despite the turbulent gale-force winds blowing forcefully against them.

CHAPTER FOUR

Designing Management Systems for Resilience

It isn't that they can't see the solution. It's that they can't see the problem.

— G. K. Chesterton, *The Scandal of Father Brown*[1]

WE ARE LIVING through a time when venerable companies—Lehman Brothers, Bear Stearns, and twenty-two banks that failed in 2008 alone—have been deleted as if they were typos in a roughly drafted letter.[2] Business leaders must have the courage to ask the hard questions, and even more courage to accept the harsh answers.

Human nature is inherently averse to taking on the risks associated with venturing into the unknown, or even worse, the unpleasant. At the same time, we do accept and take risks every day, no matter how devastating an outcome may be—usually because the worst outcomes are very rare events. For example, millions of people travel by air each day. When the flight crew gives instructions that "in the unlikely event of cabin decompression or water landing . . .," most people don't seriously contemplate what to do in the case of such an emergency, so they remain emotionally and intellectually detached from the very thought of such devastating events. While the information provided is vital to surviving such an emergency, there is an unpleasant, even slightly irrational feeling that the process of learning how to survive an emergency somehow elevates its probability. Emotions aside, in business, as in life generally, to thrive you must first learn how to survive.

Business leaders and their executive staffs will be charged with ensuring that chaotics behaviors and strategies are infused and embedded into the organization. With the *Chaotics Management System,* we present not a customized strategy into which every business enterprise must fit but a customizable framework of strategic behaviors. This framework is adaptive in its usability, as the variables of each business enterprise are inherently specific and unique.

Whether business leaders believe the new environment presents more opportunities or threats, increasing turbulence is now a fact of business life. The most effective way of dealing with the new reality is with a pragmatic, highly disciplined approach—an approach of well-defined systems designed around a robust, resilient, and responsive management framework upon which each key business operation should be based. In this way, business leaders mitigate the chances of being taken by surprise during times of crisis, as Citicorp and General Motors have been, and having to scramble to keep their companies from catastrophic disruption and even collapse.

Before imposing any broad cuts in their spending, leaders need to identify inefficiencies existent in one or more of their key functional departments: finance and information technology, manufacturing and operations, purchasing and procurement, human resources, and others. In normal times, these inefficiencies are tolerated. But in turbulent times, these inefficiencies (the "fat") can make such companies particularly vulnerable. Their old business models will not work in the turbulent situation and they must begin to reallocate their capital to their better products, segments, and geographies or risk losing their capital.

"Top business leaders who make aggressive moves now can enhance their positions in the medium and long term," says Mike Hunter, the president of management consultancy Hunter-Wells LLC. A twenty-five-year veteran dealing with fast-changing business conditions all over the world, he advises companies in marketing and sales strategy. "The short term is what it is—uncertain—so you must deal with it intelligently," says Hunter. He goes on to say, "Take, for instance, one client [who] is tightening up distribution channels by eliminating weaker players and increasing support for the stronger ones; in another case we're realigning a client's sales and marketing strategies by increasing marketing investment measurement and accountability—nothing like a good financial crisis to foster cooperation between warring factions; and with another client we've restructured their product management and portfolio management processes, eliminating wasteful investments on nonperforming products while freeing development time to focus on new, reengineered products to launch into the Chinese market by mid-2009."

Hunter sums it all up by stating that "all of these moves save money *and* they all have significant upside revenue potential. These companies get it. They're sniffing out opportunities under gray skies and they understand that bold—yet intelligent—investments made today can radically change the competitive landscape tomorrow."

Business leaders need to recognize that the environment is now changing in ways that are becoming increasingly difficult to predict. To capitalize on the new turbulent environment, companies must steadily grow more *responsive, robust,* and *resilient* or otherwise risk

failure. Such is the purpose for implementing a chaotics management system. Business leaders need to confront the inevitability of
economic turbulence and chaos head-on and to do so boldly by
developing new strategic behaviors—*chaotics behaviors*—for each
of the key functional departments. In the typical business enterprise, as shown in Figure 4–1, these key departments are finance
(including information technology); manufacturing/operations;
marketing and sales; procurement; and human resources. Chaotics
behaviors for marketing and sales functions will be discussed sep-
arately in Chapter 5.

The goal is for business leaders to create organizations that are
responsive, robust, and *resilient*—in short, organizations that have
the ability to live and thrive. These are organizations that aspire to
and attain Business Enterprise Sustainability (BES), which will be
discussed in detail in Chapter 6.

Simple, straightforward definitions of each of these three characteristics—responsiveness, robustness, and resilience—provide
insight into the goal of all business leaders:[3]

- Being *responsive* is the quality of being able to quickly react
  to external stimuli.

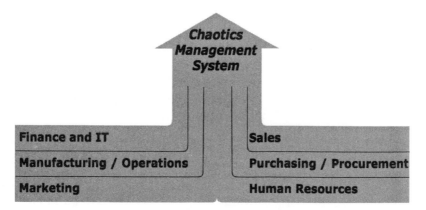

Figure 4–1. *Designing management and marketing systems for resiliency.*

- Being *robust* is the quality of being able to withstand stresses, pressures, or changes in procedure or circumstance; it means being capable of coping well with variations (sometimes unpredictable variations) in operating environments with minimal damage, alteration, or loss of functionality.

- Being *resilient* is the quality of being able to return to an original form or position after being bent, compressed, or stretched; in business, it means being able to spring back or rebound.

When we speak of companies that succeed year after year in adjusting to changing environments, among them are the "hidden champions" first discussed by Hermann Simon, founder and managing director of the respected global management consulting firm, Simon-Kucher & Partners, in his book *Hidden Champions: Lessons from 500 of the World's Best Unknown Companies*.[4] Simon has continued his study of hidden champions in his latest book, *Hidden Champions of the Twenty-First Century*.[5] He has built a database of more than 2,000 hidden champion companies not well known to the general public, but which are very profitable. These companies are found in all parts of the world, with a concentration in Europe and North America. Simon defines hidden champions as midsize companies that are usually engaged in business-to-business activities. They are highly focused, at the top in their class in quality, customer closeness, and innovation, often with regional or global operations. Moreover, they are highly profitable companies that are either number one in their continent serving that market, or number one, two, or three in the global market.

Simon summarized the hidden champions' "nine lessons" in a systems context in three nested circles. Two of the "nine lessons" that are essential to the hidden champions' business core are: (1) strong leadership, and (2) ambitious goals. Three of the nine lessons that are bound to internal capabilities include: (3) reliance on own strength, (4) continuous innovation, and (5) selected and motivated employees. Then the last four of Simon's nine lessons that characterize hidden champions' ability to drive their external opportunities include (6) narrow market focus, (7) competitive advantages, (8) closeness to the customer, and (9) global orientation.

Like Simon's hidden champions that recognize that the environment is now changing in more ways that are impossible to predict, all companies must steadily grow more responsive, robust, and resilient in this new environment. The goal of a chaotics management system is, once again, to help businesses acquire the traits that will help them survive and thrive and ultimately attain Business Enterprise Sustainability.

Simon's hidden champions model is similar to the model suggested by the evolutionist Stephen Jay Gould. In his so-called "punctuated equilibria" theory,[6] Gould asserted that evolution is not a continuous process, but rather occurs in leaps. There are long periods with minimal mutations, followed by brief phases with abrupt changes. This hypothesis could well apply to markets in general and to the hidden champions in particular. A majority of those questioned by Simon confirm that the development of their company proceeded in distinctive leaps.[7] To this end, one might suspect that the current phase of rapid globalization and dramatic changes in the global economic landscape is putting the hidden champions of the twenty-first century into a position in which they are advancing their growth and their market share fast and decisively—or have done so already.

The Chaotics Management System

From the very first chapter, we have outlined the necessary steps for business executives to begin to transition and create a sustainable business enterprise capable of withstanding stress even in the most

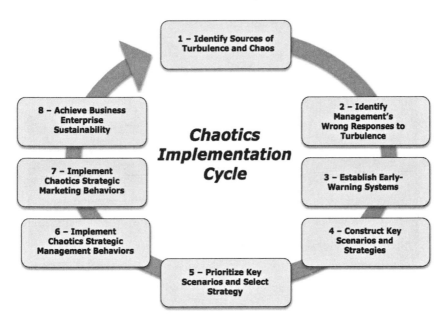

Figure 4–2. Chaotics implementation cycle.

tumultuous environments. Each chapter provides a step-by-step process to ensure that companies overall and their key departments are prepared to act quickly and decisively in the face of unexpected turbulence. To provide a clear roadmap to implement a chaotics management system, a straightforward and highly focused eight-step process is outlined here and in Figure 4–2.

Identify Sources of Turbulence and Chaos . . . . . (Chapter 1)

Identify Management's Wrong Responses
    to Turbulence . . . . (Chapter 2)

Establish Early Warning Systems . . . . (Chapter 3)

Construct Key Scenarios and Strategies. . . . . (Chapter 3)

Prioritize Key Scenarios and Select Strategy . . . . . (Chapter 3)

Implement Chaotics Strategic

Management Behaviors . . . . (Chapter 4)

Implement Chaotics Strategic

Marketing Behaviors . . . . (Chapter 5)

Achieve Business Enterprise Sustainability. . . . . . (Chapter 6)

As a further guide, we have outlined a five-step process to exe-cute *chaotics strategic behaviors* that should be applied to the organization overall, department by department, for key support systems and stakeholder groups for each of the key functional departments (see Figure 4–3). As each business works its way through each step in the execution process, it should be mindful of the continuous need to reassess and revise strategic behaviors of each department (see step 5 in Figure 4–3).

Figure 4–3. Chaotics strategic behaviors execution plan.

Step 1. Reconfirm the current business model and strategy. It is necessary to review one's business model and strategies, especially in turbulent times. When the process to adopt and adapt new strategic behaviors begins, it is absolutely fundamental that the business models and the strategies are the right ones.

Step 2. Assess the organization's ability to execute strategy under chaos. If a business has never had to experience how its organization functions under high levels of chaos, it has been very lucky, and it's been living on borrowed time. One top executive relayed this story: When the roof of his company's biggest production facility collapsed under the weight of a "once in a century" snowfall on the U.S. East Coast, there were no plans in place to reallocate production to the company's other two North American production facilities. Within twenty-four hours, at least half of the company's top customers weren't getting the products they needed, as lean manufacturing was proudly installed a year earlier and inventory stocks were cost-efficiently low. Within the next twenty-four hours, the same top executive's team had contracted with three separate contract manufacturers to fill the gap for the next three months before the damaged facility came back online. While this top executive and his team get a "C" for failing to construct key scenarios, they get an "A" for their ability to function under chaos. Needless to say, they have since fully implemented chaotics strategic behaviors to minimize big surprises—or at least adapt quickly in the event of a big surprise.

Step 3. Define the strategic behaviors execution processes. Here's where most of the hard work gets done to create the new strategic behaviors. Once there are benchmarks to understand the internal and extended organization (e.g., key stakeholders), review all elements of the organization necessary for executing strategic behaviors. That includes all groups assessed in step 2; any systems and processes within the organization; performance measurements modified as needed to ensure that objectives are met; new skills training provided as needed to execute the new behaviors; new cross-functional decision-making platforms for fast-response teams; and finally, commitment from executive management to drive through all the necessary change actions and provide the funding to get it all done.

Step 4. Execute the chaotics strategic behaviors. At this point, new strategic behaviors should be implemented in the company's key departments and throughout the entire extended organization. These behaviors need to be tested and retested for quick and effective deployment.

Step 5. Reassess and revise. Finally, it is important to remember that as the state of the new normality is punctuated by spurts of prosperity and downturn, the levels of chaos will rise and fall over time, and sometimes the chaos will reach strategic inflection points that will demand a company's business model be dissolved so it can morph into a new one. Even short of reaching these game-changing strategic inflection points, the old business model and its accompanying strategies need to be reassessed and revised on a continuous basis by business leaders and their executive staffs, as shown in the single closed loop in Figure 4–3.

Drawing on the experiences of a wide range of companies that have perennially outperformed their industry counterparts, let's turn our attention to how some key functional departments should begin to create more responsive, robust, and resilient organizations. Let's examine what the CEO should expect each department to do in response to new outbreaks of turbulence and chaos.

Finance and Information Technology
FINANCE
As *Economist* magazine stated when the financial meltdown of 2008 swung into full gear, "Prepare for the year of the finance director.

The world will continue to find out just how bad corporate balance sheets really are, and companies—most of which escaped the early effects of the credit crunch—will start to find it trickier to raise money. Add to that the upward push in costs and downward slide in demand, and the chief financial officer (CFO) will be called upon to shore up the P & L, too."[8]

When CFOs and IT executives see that the economy or their industry is in for an extended rocky period, they can look to a concise checklist of strategic behaviors developed solely for their departments to guide them through the areas in which they need to take action to Cut/Delay, Outsource, or Increase/Accelerate, as shown in Figure 4–4). This checklist for chaotics behaviors for financial and information technology is a simple and concise tool that gives financial and IT executives a place to begin as they prepare to head into extended periods of disrupted normality. Many strategic behaviors are actually sections in a business plan that will require more detailed developments.

For example, one of the recommended actions is to "Increase/ Accelerate any reorganizations yielding substantial productivity gains." This recommendation covers small and large companies, regardless of the size of the challenge. One case in point is BP, the international oil giant that was close to bankruptcy during the recession in the mid-1990s when Lord (John) Browne, then head of the company's oil-exploration division (known as BPX), set out to restructure his fiefdom. The choice was stark: radical change or extermination. Accountability and responsibility for performance at BPX were pushed down to the individual oil field level. Previously, performance measures were aggregated by geographic region, leaving managers further down the line with little idea of how well they were doing and with little incentive to do better. When early experiments with disaggregation showed that it increased output and brought down costs, it was introduced across

CUT / DELAY	OUTSOURCE	INCREASE / ACCELERATE
▪ New financing relationships (unless current ones are unreliable, then cautiously seek new)	▪ All or as many noncore support services as possible	▪ New management reporting systems designed to provide decision makers with more real-time, higher-quality information
▪ IPO	▪ All or as many noncore IT services as possible	▪ New technology that enhances communications and productivity
▪ Infrastructure investments and other capital equipment expenditures	▪ All or as many noncore HR services as possible (e.g., payroll, training, compensation planning, etc.)	▪ Expense control procedures
▪ Price increases		▪ Prepayment discounts, volume discounts
▪ Favorable terms for some customers		▪ Consolidation of administrative and support expenses not yet outsourced
▪ Dividends		▪ Negotiations for more favorable terms with professional services providers (e.g., CPAs, etc.)
▪ Stock buybacks		
▪ Underperforming operations		
▪ Use of overdrafts (can be pulled by banks)		▪ Use of telepresence and teleconferencing throughout entire organization and with all stakeholders
▪ Across-the-board cuts		▪ Use of term loans (cannot be pulled by banks)
▪ Layoffs/redundancies of key employees		▪ Personal visits to all company locations with all key personnel
▪ Discretionary pension plan funding		▪ Growth via acquisition when asset prices/valuations are low
▪ Debt-to-equity (D/E) ratios vs. competitors		▪ Any reorganizations yielding substantial productivity gains

Figure 4–4. Chaotics strategic behaviors checklist for finance and information technology.

BPX, and then across the whole of BP after Lord Browne became CEO of the company in 1995.[9]

Traditionally, the oil giant had a highly centralized hierarchical structure, but Lord Browne cut its headquarters staff by some 80 percent and pushed decision making down to ninety newly established business units. The hierarchy was flattened so much that the head of each of the ninety units reported directly to the company's nine-man executive committee—though as BP subsequently grew through takeover, some intermediate layers were reintroduced. Individual managers also had much of their headquarters support removed. The top of their silo had suddenly been lopped off! To discourage the silo mentality further, horizontal links were set up between the units. BPX's assets were split into four groups, roughly reflecting the stage they had reached in their economic life. Members of each group thus faced similar commercial and technical issues and were encouraged to support others in their group and help solve each other's problems. BP's people developed a deep, intrinsic dedication to delivering ever-improving performance. Strong norms of mutual trust emerged—norms that included admitting early when one faced difficulties and seeking assistance when needed, and responding positively to requests for help, and keeping promises about performance. As part of the forced reorganization during the most difficult of economic times, some assets were sold off and BP's total staff was cut by almost 50 percent in just three years, with much improved financial performance for the next decade.[10]

Lord Browne's actions at BP in the 1990s were right in line with more recent findings from a McKinsey study report on the 2000–2001 recession: When entering downturns, the most successful CFOs typically maintain lower leverage on their balance sheets and keep tight control over their operating costs. Such fundamentals give them a greater degree of strategic flexibility, which becomes even more valuable during recession. And although previous recessions aren't necessarily a guide to future ones, the McKinsey study participants believe that flexibility can make a notable difference by allowing CFOs to take advantage of the opportunities that the next recession might provide.

The McKinsey study found that the most successful CFOs gained critical flexibility for their firms. Specifically, their flexibility was highlighted in the balance sheet and in operations, as follows:[11]

Balance Sheet Flexibility

- Steady increases in capacity:

  - Continue and increase capacity organically.

- Reduction in inventories and also payables:

  - Maintain lean inventories; continue to improve levels pre-recession.

  - Maintain ability to pay suppliers sooner to secure better contract terms.

- Financing capacity for taking advantage of opportunities:

  - Reduce leverage compared with industry peers.

  - Boost ability to finance internally through higher cash balance, lower dividends.

Operating Flexibility

- Cost variability:

  - Reduce selling, general, and administrative costs during recession.

  - Build ability to quickly refocus to reduce spending.

  - Maintain higher employee productivity.

  - Make no across-the-board headcount reductions.

Regardless how these companies were positioned before the downturn, many that emerged as leaders managed to expand their businesses during the recession, both organically (through internal investment) and through inorganic activities such as mergers and acquisitions, alliances, and joint ventures. And although the leaders increased their asset bases through capital expenditures or acquisitions at the same pace as less successful companies, the focus of their growth was different: The more successful CFOs made sure their companies spent less on M&A activities, on average, and focused more on organic growth during times of growth and prosperity.[12]

The McKinsey study reported that leading companies had, on average, capital expenditures that were 8 percent higher and growth through M&A that was 13 percent lower than their less successful counterparts. During the recession itself, however, better performers leapfrogged the competition by continuing to invest and to grow inorganically: Companies that emerged in the top quartile spent 15 percent more on capital expenditures and conducted 7 percent more M&A—possibly buying cheaper assets from distressed sellers. These CFOs were also able to pay their suppliers faster to negotiate lower prices and better service. Winning CFOs also leveraged the benefits of their firm's balance sheet flexibility that they had achieved before the recession and ultimately emerged as sector leaders. For example, average net debt-to-equity (D/E) ratio before the recession was half that of their less successful competitors, and post-recession leaders held more cash on their balance sheets prior to the recession than those emerging less successfully.[13]

CFOs can build flexibility into a company's balance sheet by reducing the capital intensity of the business model, for example, or by resisting the urge to use additional debt to finance dividend growth or share buybacks. In the same McKinsey study, as profits grew during the expansion, the companies that emerged as winners refrained from increasing their dividends: Their dividend payout ratio gradually decreased from a peak of 40 percent to 32 percent four years later. Then they cut dividend payouts aggressively at the first signs of the recession, reducing the payout ratio to 28 percent. In contrast, before the recession their less successful counterparts kept dividend payouts roughly stable—at 33 percent over the same periods—and even increased them to an average 38 percent as the last recession began.[14]

The prospect of a prolonged downturn should lead to CFOs introducing more severe contingency plans for managing credit risk, freeing up cash, selling assets, and reassessing growth. But executives should also think through the opportunities that a downturn provides. Research shows that at the start of a downturn—when costs such as capital expenditures, R & D, and advertising are high—executives who have planned in advance on cuts or on expansion can make the right moves.

A downturn, especially an extended one, can be a great opportunity to hire new top talent while being sure to retain the talent currently in the company. It is also a time to continue spending on long-term strategic initiatives and to target strategic acquisitions, especially acquisitions of businesses that may have been on the radar screen but were too pricey to buy during more prosperous economic times. Companies that now enjoy strong balance sheets have a good position to take advantage of current credit market conditions and reap outsize value for shareholders.

Regrettably, there are many functions within the realm of the CFO's responsibility that are non-value-adding; not because the CFO doesn't add value, but because the services are still performed in-house. Some of these support services should be immediately outsourced because they provide the CFO high leverage for all times. For example:

Function:	Outsource to:
Payroll and payroll taxes	Payroll services firm
Employee benefits	Plan administrators
Publications	Fulfillment firms
Conference planning	Conference planning firms
Facilities management	External agent firms depending upon function
Investments	External asset managers

In many cases, building in financial and operational flexibility forms the core of the CFO's efforts to benefit from a downturn. Executives must therefore understand how to make costs more variable, and CFOs need to understand how to get their balance sheets ready. The desirable moves include shaping the investor base to generate support for ideas that might seem to go against conventional wisdom in a downturn and could require a dividend reduction.

Successful past experience by companies that weathered the worst of economic storms points to the fact that companies should be very cautious about developing new financing relationships during chaotic times. During tough times, companies need to stay very close with their most reliable and trusted banking and investor partners. However, this is not the case for all companies, as some may have such partners who've become unreliable. Companies that need more reliable and resilient financial partners shouldn't rule out investigating and approaching potential new ones, such as private-equity players or sovereign wealth funds, whose resources could help their allies make the most of a slump, who have demonstrated a mindset more aligned with the mid-term and the long-term, and who could be more reliable than current partners.

When difficult economic times approach, business executives begin to ask their senior executives to prepare their departments for the rough ride ahead. Going forward, these rough rides will be for longer periods. Some questions that may be put to a CFO include:

- What steps are we taking to reduce overall costs?

- What is our cash flow situation like, and what are you doing to preserve it?

- What major capital expenditures that we've got coming up can we delay?

- What is the status of our lines of credit with our banks, and can they be tapped easily?

- What can we do to increase margins on our product lines across the board?

And there will be many more questions. CFOs will need to be ready to answer these difficult questions for themselves long before they are posed by their CEOs.

INFORMATION TECHNOLOGY

During both difficult and expansive economic times, IT executives should always look for ways to trim spending and improve the bottom line. "The knee-jerk reaction is to pull back into the comfort zone, press the pause buttons, and cut costs," says Brian Murray, technology strategist for the Morse Group consultancy. He says such a tactic can be a false economy—that is, the action may save money at the beginning, but over a longer period of time, it results in more money being wasted than being saved. As the overall picture gets complex, exacerbated by the speed and depth of the downturn, most companies react hastily. According to a Gartner Group client affected by the global recession, "They just tore up the budget that was barely two weeks old and were starting from scratch."[15]

According to recent studies, when business executives and IT executives jointly take an end-to-end look at business processes, the resulting investments can have up to ten times the impact of traditional IT cost-reduction efforts. Downturns give companies a chance to buck conventional wisdom and increase their IT investments. Targeted investments in many areas can generate efficiencies and revenue growth that surpass the savings from straight cost reductions.

The trick is to scan for opportunities—such as improving the customer experience, reducing revenue leakage, and improving operating leverage. Such an effort begins with a survey of manufacturing and operations, to identify areas likely to produce near-term revenue and efficiency gains, and then you identify ways IT investments can have a substantial impact, according to one 2008 study from McKinsey.[16] For example:

- *Manage sales and pricing.* Develop insights into customer segments and improve pricing discipline to increase revenues without increasing prices.

- *Optimize sourcing and production.* Rethink supply chains and logistics to improve the scheduling of deliveries and inventory management.

- *Enhance support processes.* Improve the management and use of field forces (such as installers and field technicians) and of customer support centers.

- *Optimize overhead and performance management.* Sharpen awareness of risk exposure and improve decision-making and performance-management processes.

Manufacturing/Operations

With the right foresight, planning, and action, many manufacturing and operations executives may be able to position their companies not only to survive any economic downturns but to benefit in the long run because the new environment forces long-overdue changes to processes, including the control systems that drive significant costs in their businesses. The first step in preventing economic downturns from cutting into profits is to conduct a stringent analysis to streamline your company's cost structure without cutting into the high-value parts of the operation. An organization's administrative and operational infrastructure tends to grow slowly and on a selective basis in good economic conditions, but when business falls off it usually receives quick scrutiny and is subject to swift across-the-board reductions.

Manufacturing and operations executives understand that their companies' cost structure is essential for reducing or eliminating costs that don't impact sales. Because marketing, sales, and customer and technical service support staffs are involved in indirect expenses on a day-to-day basis, they are excellent resources for identifying wasteful and inefficient practices. Going forward in a more collaborative and cross-functional approach is the best way to identify and eliminate non-value-adding direct expenses and reduce newly unnecessary indirect expenses.[17]

Unfortunately, during a deep economic downturn, some hard decisions need to be made. The most obvious way to cut costs is to reduce staffing. Management needs to determine which workers add critical value and which do not. One could argue that the entire staff provides critical value. In this case, which members add the least? Are there areas where responsibilities clearly overlap? If so, one person may need to fill the shoes of two while the company weathers the economic storm. Those workers that add the most critical value and are not in the firing line should be informed of their value to the company to maintain morale levels.

When manufacturing and operations executives are asked what their groups can do to help their firms weather difficult times, they can now look to a checklist of strategic behaviors developed for their departments to take the necessary actions (see Figure 4–5). This checklist for chaotics behaviors for manufacturing/operations should be applied during all times. The only exception may be during an extended spurt of prosperity. However, even then, the early-warning system must operate to detect any fresh developments that may hit a company.

Employee morale in manufacturing/operations is crucial to ensuring that productivity remains strong and the corporate environment upbeat. It is very important that you ensure worker participation by including them in communications so that they know what is going on.[18] This is an ideal time for additional training. Cross-training boosts productivity and flexibility as it allows workers to "cover" for one another in the event of an illness, vacation, or termination. This investment in extra training also provides deserving workers with extra responsibilities, which, in turn, increases their self-motivation.

When projected sales decrease during an economic downturn, production levels need to drop proportionally. This is not the time to tie up working capital in excess inventory. Management must identify costs that vary with production level and ensure that those costs are reduced appropriately. Pay attention to the warning sign of excessive production: a steady inventory increase as measured by the number of day sales in inventory.

In a paper entitled "The Strategic Enterprise: Rethinking the Design of Complex Organizations," Mercer Delta Consulting describes its vision of the organizational architecture of the future: strategically aligned businesses linked closely where there are

CUT / DELAY	OUTSOURCE	INCREASE / ACCELERATE
■ Capacity-related capital expenditure projects (exception: company has high cash reserves and high ROI projects)	■ Design and engineering work that is not critical to competitive advantage	■ Incentives for unions and vendors that identify significant cost-saving opportunities
■ New supplier relationships; instead, work to keep current suppliers viable	■ Production requiring new technology or new equipment	■ Bonuses for productivity gains
■ Unnecessary steps in manufacturing process (e.g., extra packaging material, paint, hardware)	■ Low value production	■ Functional cross-training for increased operator flexibility
■ Shipment schedules	■ Logistics and supply chain management	■ Investment in plant throughput initiatives
■ Inventories, but without jeopardizing customer service with core customers		■ Cross-facility collaboration
■ New product or enhancements to noncore products and services		■ Investment in technology to improve communication and accountability
		■ SKU rationalization
		■ Overtime until new hiring must be initiated
		■ Accuracy of production forecasts
		■ Inventory turns

Figure 4–5. Chaotics strategic behaviors checklist for manufacturing/operations.

opportunities to create value by leveraging shared capabilities, but only loosely where the greater value lies in differentiated focus. In other words, close and loose relationships will coexist within the same organization. For example, within R&D, a close cross-functional relationship between two firms may be beneficial to both. Conversely, if a different function, let's say the marketing function, within these same two businesses cannot readily provide reciprocal added value to each other, then this part of the relationship between the two firms will be loose.

In the traditional organizational structure, units were either within the organization and, as Mercer Delta's David Nadler puts it, "densely connected," or they were outside the organization and not connected at all. Transactions with external suppliers were at arm's length. By contrast, companies today cohabit with a vast number of joint ventures and strategic alliances, some more and some less connected. The line between what is inside and what is outside the corporation, once so clear, has become blurred.[19]

One of the most contentious of these new relationships is outsourcing—the handing over to others of what were once considered to be core functions of the company. First to be transferred to more efficient providers were companies' manufacturing operations. Some firms have stretched outsourcing to such an extent that they now make nothing. All of Nike's shoes are manufactured by subcontractors. The company employs few people directly. Rather than manufacture products, such companies now orchestrate brands. Like a conductor whose baton has only limited control over the individual musicians in the orchestra, such a company can still deliver a great product. Even Procter & Gamble—the quintessential manufacturer—has joined the bandwagon. "Our core capability is to develop and commercialize," P&G's chief executive, A. G. Lafley, has said. "We concluded in a lot of areas that manufacturing isn't [a core capability]. Therefore I let the businesses go do more outsourcing."[20]

During a downturn, management should use a multifaceted approach to maintain or even increase company margins. One of management's top priorities should be to build consistency in production and labor policies across the organization. If variable costs do not decrease in direct proportion to production decreases, management is failing to do its job. Essential to addressing such inconsistencies, the entire operation must be aligned toward common goals using common metrics. Make sure to review performance indicators to ensure that they are appropriate measures of your progress toward your goals.[21]

Having identified the common behaviors of manufacturing and operations executives from companies that continually weather extended periods of economic turbulence we recommend the following ten practices:[22]

- *Move quickly to reduce costs and control spending by narrowing the business focus.* Winners focus on a few critical priorities where they can develop a clear lead; they walk away from bad business. Losers in a downturn chase unprofitable sales in an attempt to hold their top line.

- *Refrain from across-the-board operations cutbacks.* Be sure to preserve areas that customers value most. Businesses that uniformly cut costs often end up damaging their ability to deliver their products and services. How do you find out what customers value most? Ask them.

- *Consider alternatives to layoffs.* Downsizing tends to bolster the bottom line and stock price in the short term, but it often creates negative repercussions in the long term. Alternative strategies include cutting management bonuses, freezing salaries, and reducing compensation options. Clearly communicate the rationale and impact of any of these measures to employees.

- *Invest in opportunity.* A bad economy can present bargains, both in new assets and in new talent. Other good areas to invest are in R&D, marketing, and customer-perceived quality. By contrast, investing in working capital, manufacturing, and administration doesn't pay off as well.

- *Retain and develop top talent.* High-impact workers are often more susceptible to being poached by a competitor in a downturn. Organizations that provide development experiences and rotational assignments have better employee retention rates.

- *Make sure everyone's on the same page.* According to studies on strategy execution, performance suffers when alignment on key goals is absent. Top leaders frame an agenda and meet with key stakeholders to gain support and build commitment to overarching goals and values. Ineffective leaders let interoffice politics fester and hidden agendas dominate.

- *Encourage questions and new ideas.* Make it safe for employees to raise questions and offer suggestions. Successful leaders who admit they don't have all the answers and ask for input empower their people to contribute their best ideas.

- *Manage the heat.* Manufacturing and operations executives are often tempted in difficult times to relieve the organization's stress by making unilateral, tough decisions. That can be a mistake. Leadership by dictate doesn't often work. It lacks a broad base of support, and it tends to eliminate constructive conflicts that challenge the status quo and fuel good decision making.

- *Communicate authentically.* Strong leaders acknowledge their challenges. In doing so, they build trust. Rather than being a sign of weakness, it is a sign of strength.

■ *Create a positive vision and attitude that acknowledges reality.* The topple rate can victimize any company that doesn't stay on top of its game. Businesses at the top of their markets very often fall while the more aggressive and motivated companies jump to the top in a tough economy. When manufacturing and operations executives exercise discipline and mobilize their employees to respond to customers' interests and values, they increase the chance that, when the downturn ends, they'll come out on top.

When manufacturing executives are confronted with difficult economic times, here are some of the questions they may be asked:

■ What can be done to reduce our costs through greater production efficiencies?

■ What can be done to get the fixed overhead down through the downturn?

■ What functions in operations can we outsource to get costs down?

■ What can we do to cut R & D costs? Should we be adding to R & D?

■ What can we do to get everyone in production on board with cost reductions?

And there will be many more questions, especially because most product companies have a large, capital-intensive asset base. Once a proud collection of prized trophies, production facilities for more and more companies are increasingly becoming an anchor weighing down their ability to be agile and adaptive. Manufacturing and operations executives must therefore be ready to answer these difficult questions for themselves long before their CEOs ask them.

Purchasing/Procurement

For more than a decade of relentless competition fueled by globalization, business executives have been aware of the strategic benefits achievable through the intelligent use of purchasing and supply management. At the same time, there is a grudging acknowledgment that relatively few companies have truly exploited all, or even most, of the gains available from these functions, especially as many companies are now quickly scrambling to reduce purchasing costs (that's code for "getting suppliers to cut their prices") during the ensuing chaotic times in their industries and businesses. The main concerns include more competitive supply chains, improved product development, and faster time to market—in addition to the significant cost advantages associated with sourcing from low-cost countries, which for some industries may even include the United States. Yet the evolution in the way executives think about purchasing hasn't translated into the results they seek. A shortage of strategic behaviors too often derails the improvement efforts of many companies, while others suffer from a misalignment between purchasing and the broader company strategy.

When difficult economic times begin to approach, business executives ask their senior executives to prepare their departments for the difficulties ahead. Questions for purchasing and procurement executives may include:

- What technologies can we use to get a better view of our loaded purchasing costs?

- What top-ten categories are available for cost reduction, and how much can we expect to save in each category?

- What additional value can we extract from our suppliers to reduce our costs?

- Should we be considering new suppliers to replace higher-cost ones?

- What services should we be outsourcing, how do we do it, and much can we save?

Purchasing executives can look to a checklist of strategic behaviors developed for their departments, as shown in Figure 4–6.

For many companies, the role of purchasing hasn't evolved much beyond the function's narrow transactional roots as a buyer of materials, components, and services. But some purchasing and supply-management organizations are attracting the attention of CEOs by taking the function to the next level. Procurement's tactical potential as a cost killer is no secret. After all, spending on purchased goods and services can represent a significant percentage of a company's costs, so business leaders have long known that purchasing improvements can directly improve the bottom line.

According to another McKinsey report, top purchasers adopt a more rigorous approach to talent by simultaneously upgrading their procurement skills and exploring clever ways to connect employees across the organization in a common purpose. These companies also set high aspirations and establish goals that balance their vision of the future with a clear-eyed focus on how to achieve it. Finally, top purchasers place a special emphasis on aligning their sourcing efforts more closely with corporate strategic goals, pursuing today's cost-savings opportunities while positioning themselves for greater gains as globalization intensifies. These pioneering organizations are laying the foundation for a better approach to procurement—an approach that average performers shouldn't ignore."[23]

To help assist purchasing and procurement executives who need to elevate their game during difficult economic times when relationships between companies and their suppliers may become strained, here are ten key practices for effective purchasing. These practices were developed by some of the world's top purchasing

CUT / DELAY	OUTSOURCE	INCREASE / ACCELERATE
■ Capacity-related capital expenditure projects, even those with high ROI ■ New supplier relationships; instead, work to keep current key suppliers viable ■ Use of nonkey suppliers	■ Design and engineering work that is not critical to competitive advantage ■ Production requiring new technology or new equipment	■ Knowledge of all key suppliers ■ Improvements to key supplier relationships ■ Communications to key suppliers ■ Joint supplier audits ■ Supply chain optimization ■ Incentives for unions and suppliers (and other stakeholders) to identify cost savings, productivity gains, and revenue enhancement opportunities ■ Cross-functional training for increased production flexibility ■ Training of purchasing staff ■ Internal compliance with preferred purchasing lists ■ Price hedging contracts

Figure 4–6. Chaotics strategic behaviors checklist for purchasing/procurement.

gurus from organizations that were recently named *Purchasing* magazine's best companies:[24]

1. *Improve supplier relations.* Avoid supplier relationships that are too cozy or too adversarial. Order in a manner that keeps suppliers' cost low to reduce costs. Work with the best suppliers, taking into account local, regional, national, and global players for the goods and services you need. For companies working with too many suppliers, find a great supplier or two and gain leverage by giving them all or most of the business. Develop an annual cost reduction plan; the best suppliers will understand this concept.

2. *Develop a scorecard for keeping track of suppliers' service, quality, delivery, and pricing.* Track the quality, service, and price performance of suppliers, and then communicate your scorecard results to them. Understand what is important to suppliers, and make sure they understand what is important to you. When possible, involve suppliers in the product design from the very beginning.

3. *Obtain the right information.* Rightsize the number of suppliers you use. Leverage volume with suppliers. Purchasing and finance should form a team to identify current spending as well as opportunities for improvement. Engineering, manufacturing, and sales should be included to brainstorm ideas for product and process improvements.

4. *Create a purchasing staff with the right skills.* You want staff with analytical skills to get into the details of what is purchased. You need people with great negotiation skills—very few purchasing executives and the buyers reporting to them are trained negotiators. Business knowledge is also vital, including an ability to understand the business goals of purchasing executives and the ability to work in other parts of the organization (e.g., sales, operations, finance) to assist them in achieving their goals. Furthermore, understanding the focus of your suppliers' businesses is critical to making sure the purchasing staff can provide necessary assistance to help suppliers reach their goals, too.

5. *Get the executive team behind purchasing 100 percent.* Top purchasing executives should report to the CEO or COO, not be stuck behind another executive in the company. Top officials must have a direct line to purchasing so that they can understand the impact price increases will have on their business and decide whether to pass the increases on to customers. Potential price increases need to be offset with decreases in other areas. A team approach to purchasing helps to focus on the priority areas within a company.

6. *Enforce a preferred supplier list.* Purchasing executives should support the purchasing managers when a tough decision must be made on changing suppliers. A preferred supplier list will prevent a total supplier list from getting out of control.

7. *Structure teams that are centrally led, but locally implemented.* To obtain the best leverage available, purchasing executives should gather data in a central point to evaluate total spending by area. Once the total spend by area is determined, purchasing teams should be created to identify the best suppliers for those areas. Increase the amount of common commodities and supplies purchased by headquarters to gain higher volume and lower prices. Collaborate with the selected suppliers and listen to their ideas for achieving greater success.

8. *Develop strong negotiation strategies.* Enforce evergreen clauses—organizations are burned every day by agreements that force them to use a supplier for another year, despite the desire to switch to a new one. Ongoing training and organizational development in the area of negotiation is also key to developing a win-win relationship with your supplier network.

9. *Use technology to propel ahead of the competition.* Make sure you use technology that will automate the complex tasks that used to be handled manually. Capture the correct data and tap into it when you begin a negotiation.

10. *Design an incentive program that actually profits the individual and the company.* Incentives paid to employees are critical to the ability of organizations to accept and embrace change. Make sure that what gets rewarded is what gets done.

Human Resources

During a downturn, projects are canceled, some staff members lose their jobs, and morale begins to suffer. CEOs are looking to HR executives to keep everything on track during these downturns. Getting the most out of employees in this kind of environment can seem like an impossible task, which is why so much is now asked of HR executives. In fact, it is a perfect opportunity to reset the processes and fix what's broken—and many top managers are uniquely positioned to do just that if the HR executive can show them how. Here's how being honest and open with your employees, rewarding them in creative ways, and enlisting them to help make hard decisions not only keeps organizations motivated but pulls companies out of their slumps.

When HR executives need to do more to help their firms weather the difficult times, they should also refer to the checklist of strategic behaviors developed for their department (see Figure 4–7).

Here are ten effective HR recommendations to help keep companies moving forward when the economy isn't:[25]

1. *Keep recruiting.* Most of the time, economic downturns are short-lived, so keep the bigger picture of long-term growth in sight. It is easier to invest training time for new recruits during slower growth periods. It is also worth remembering that if you dismiss employees during a recession, you may eventually have to rehire when times get better—and that can cost a lot more money in the long run.

2. *Don't recruit a problem.* During tough times, don't compromise your recruiting standards—in fact, elevate them. There will be plenty of talented people available, so your company doesn't have to settle for anyone less talented.

3. *Apportion your resources wisely.* Eliminate meetings that don't add value. Shorten the meetings. Organize sales or other company meetings with a clearly defined profit purpose. Create specific performance requirements. However, consider adding some high-impact meetings with customers or dealers when the rest of the business world is cutting back.

4. *Keep talking.* Be honest with employees about difficult times; let them understand the true financial picture. Employees are often willing to make cuts and changes when they understand the facts. Talking clearly and honestly with your employees helps to reduce the rumors flying around the workplace.

5. *Don't just rely on the CEO's message.* E-mail from the CEO explaining why the company is in the red may not tell employees much, which means mid-level managers will need to interpret. Have your managers speak to employees in small groups and be as candid as possible about where the company stands.

6. *See the silver lining.* Give employees positive feedback whenever you can. Acknowledge when a job is well done, and consider noncash incentives. It is reasonable to ask employees to do their best. If they are not performing to their full potential, a suitable performance appraisal encouraging input from both parties can be useful. Also, there's no need to sugarcoat it: Pulling the company

CUT / DELAY	OUTSOURCE	INCREASE / ACCELERATE
■ All salary increases	■ Payroll management	■ Companywide communications to keep morale high
■ Office space expansion	■ Insurance management	■ Performance-based compensation systems and bonuses
■ Companywide meetings, conventions	■ Compensation planning	■ Productivity measurements and tracking systems
■ Promotions	■ Benefits management	■ Training everyone, including executive management
■ Layoffs of key employees	■ Meetings planning	■ Use of government and community training programs
	■ Training	■ Use of contractors for training
		■ Use of computer and online interactive training
		■ Identification and retention of top talent
		■ Recruiting (but be very selective)
		■ Use of Health Savings Accounts (in the U.S.) to lower cost of health care

Figure 4–7. Chaotics strategic behaviors checklist for human resources.

through the downturn isn't going to be easy, but emphasizing the challenge can have its benefits. It's a great time for employees to realize that they can play a greater role in discovering opportunities for the company.

7. *Keep on training people.* During downturns, people need new and more advanced skills and knowledge, and training certainly provides a morale boost as well.

8. *Enlist the team to fix what's broken.* Traditionally, the top executives decide the strategy and let it trickle down. The problem with this approach is that it rarely makes the emotional case needed to mobilize employees around a common goal. This is about problem solving and discipline, and that's where employees come in. Companies should be harnessing employees in the effort to identify where and how to cut costs. Not only will employees' expertise make them more invested in the company's success, but it also gives management a more honest look at what's not working. Find the key employees who hold sway in their departments and get them to embrace and spread the change effort. These are the people who know how things really work and have a way of bringing together the right people to get things done.

9. *Follow through.* Many cost-savings programs fail because management implements the initiative only halfway or lets inefficiencies creep back after meeting short-term goals. Adopt the changes wholesale or not at all.

10. *Keep top performers moving.* In an ideal world, downturns have an upside—recruiting qualified employees becomes easier. With more candidates in the job market, now could be the time to find new talent if your company has the resources to continue hiring. But managers shouldn't forget about the top performers already on staff. When the economy's bad, it is easy to think that employees are grateful to have jobs at all. But layoffs and budget cuts may cause good workers to look for better opportunities. Give them a reason to stay by making room for them to advance their careers.

Companies' top executives must get more serious about their role in ensuring the development of the current and next generations of senior leaders at their organizations—that is, creating a deep bench of potential successors to the senior executives in each of the key functional areas, and beyond. When agendas become overcrowded, talent development is among the easiest topics to ignore or at least defer, even while no one disputes the importance of always having the right people with the right skills at the top of each business function. This is where HR executives need to step up, close the talent gap, and help their companies meet the challenges in an increasingly turbulent environment.

Conclusion

The goal of *Chaotics* is to provide business leaders with a clear guide to create responsive, robust, and resilient organizations. Such organizations have the ability to react quickly to a constantly changing environment. They can withstand great stress and pressures with minimal damage. They can cope with unpredictable variations in their environment, and they have the ability to rebound when the hard times end and circumstances improve. These enterprises will succeed in the new environment, and in *any* environment.

By boldly implementing the prophylactic protections of *chaotics strategic behaviors,* department by department, business executives will move forward to secure their companies' futures against the increasingly unpredictable environment that lies ahead. Moreover, implementing such strategic behaviors will begin the long and steady process of creating newly evolved cultures—ones in which all members are more keenly attuned to the environment and have the tools to meet with success in an uncertain future, secure their businesses from threats in the environment, and exploit new opportunities that may arise. Finally, such organizations will possess the collective knowledge and skills to create cultures that have the necessary underpinnings deeply embedded in them to attain long-term Business Enterprise Sustainability well into the future.

CHAPTER FIVE

Designing Marketing Systems for Resilience

The ones who are crazy enough to think they can change the world are the ones who do.

—Steve Jobs, Co-Founder, Chairman, and CEO, Apple, Inc.

ACCELERATING RATES of change, increasing levels of complexity, and escalating risks and uncertainty have become the new marketing reality in times of turbulence. To defend itself from the external shocks of turbulence and chaos that can destroy a business, a company must increase its capacity for resiliency at all levels, and especially in marketing and sales.

Resiliency is a mindset that marketers as well as everyone in their organization must build into themselves. Marketers need to master resiliency if they are to engage the marketplace forcefully, break through the chaos, and connect with consumers. Resilient thinking by marketers transforms anxiety into action and difficulty into decisiveness.

Great marketers don't just rebound from crises. They build the internal capacity to expect the unexpected. They continuously reinvent business models and marketing strategies during chaotic times so that they can adapt quickly as circumstances in the marketplace change.

Today, the typical company operates a marketing system that has emerged from years of trial and error. It has developed policies, strategies, and tactics for using marketing research, pricing, the sales force, advertising, promotions, trade shows, and other marketing tools. These practices are likely to persist because they deliver a feeling of safety and predictability. They worked in the past and are assumed to work in the future.

There is, however, one problem. The world keeps changing. Increasing turbulence and chaos are transforming the world faster and in more dramatic ways than any time in the past fifty years. Today, customers experience shifts in their interests, budgets, and values. Distribution channels take on new forms while new communication channels emerge. New competitors appear. New government legislation and regulation are imposed. Turbulence is ever-present.

These developments put a company at a strategic inflection point: Either the company continues with the same strategy or recognizes the need for a new one. Clearly, the company needs to revisit and revise its marketing policies and tools. If it doesn't, the new environment will punish the company—maybe to the point of failure.

The first task is to recognize the major changes that have been taking place in the marketing landscape. Four key changes are listed below. These changes call for radically new thinking by managers and marketers.

Four key changes in the marketing landscape

1. Customers are better informed than ever. They are empowered. They can find out almost anything about any product, service, or company by searching on the Internet and contacting others in their social networks.

2. Customers are increasingly ready to buy and trust well-known store brands when they are priced lower than the well-advertised national brands.

3. Competitors are able to copy faster any new product or service, thus shortening the innovator's return on investment (ROI). Competitive advantages have a much shorter life today.

4. The Internet and social networks have created radically new media and information sources, as well as new means for direct-to-customer selling.

These changes call for radically new thinking by managers and marketers. Smart companies are shifting from one way of thinking to another.

Major Shifts in the Mindsets of Marketers

- From marketers thinking about the customers to everyone in the company thinking about customers

- From selling to everyone to trying to be the best firm serving well-defined target markets

- From organizing by products to organizing by customer segments

- From making everything inside the company to buying more goods and services from outside

- From using many suppliers to working with fewer, more partner-oriented suppliers

- From emphasizing tangible assets to emphasizing intangible marketing assets (company brands, customer equity, channel loyalty, and intellectual property)

- From building brands through advertising to building brands through integrated marketing communications (IMC) and performance that satisfies

- From making profit on every sale to building long-time customer value

- From aiming for more market share to aiming for more share of each customer's wallet

- From being local to being "glocal" (both global and local)

- From focusing on the financial scorecard to also focusing on the marketing scorecard

- From focusing on shareholder benefit to focusing on stakeholder benefit

We are not saying that every company is shifting its marketing mindset. The purpose of these lists is to encourage your company to question its current marketing policies and ideas. Hopefully, you will make some important changes that will improve marketing performance.

Another stimulus to rethinking a company's marketing is to look at the characteristics that normally distinguish poor, good, and great marketing companies.

| POOR, GOOD, AND GREAT MARKETING CHARACTERISTICS | | |
Poor	Good	Great
Product driven	Market driven	Market driving
Mass-market oriented	Segment oriented	Niche oriented
Product offer	Augmented product offer	Customer solutions offer
Average product quality	Better than average	Legendary
Average service quality	Better than average	Legendary
Function oriented	Process oriented	Outcome oriented
Reacting to competitors	Benchmarking competitors	Leapfrogging competitors
Supplier exploitation	Supplier preference	Supplier partnership
Dealer exploitation	Dealer support	Dealer partnership
Price driven	Quality driven	Value driven
Average speed	Better than average	Legendary
Hierarchy	Network	Teamwork
Vertically integrated	Flattened organization	Strategic alliances
Stockholder driven	Stakeholder driven	Societal driven

Source: Philip Kotler, *Marketing Management,* 13th ed., p. 660.

Common Marketing Reactions to Crises

Whatever your company's marketing posture may be in normal times, it will change in turbulent times, especially at the onset of a downward spiral or a recession. That's because in response to the recession your customers will change their behavior and what they value.

First, consider consumers. Faced with the prospect of harder times and possibly even job loss, they will cut their spending. Here are three likely consumer behaviors:

- *Consumers move toward lower-priced products and brands.* They will replace buying national brands with store brands and even generic brands. This changed behavior will fall hard on national and international premium brands, especially the weaker higher-priced brands.

- *Consumers reduce or postpone discretionary purchases such as autos, furniture, major appliances, and expensive vacations.* Those companies that make or sell discretionary products and services will be forced to budget downward, reduce inventory, and possibly lay off workers. Suppliers and employees will be left with less purchasing power and reduce their purchases accordingly.

- *Consumers cut back on driving and start buying more from suppliers nearer to their work or home.* They will spend more time eating their meals at home and relying on in-home entertainment from TV and the Internet.

Businesses will also make moves to reduce their costs and conserve capital. They will take such steps as:

- Reducing production and ordering fewer goods from their suppliers. They don't want to build inventories in the face of falling demand. They don't want to slash prices in order to liquidate inventories.

- Cutting their rate of capital investment. This decision will hurt the demand for steel, cement, machinery, software, and many other inputs.

- Reducing their marketing budgets substantially.

- Postponing new product development and putting major new projects on hold.

One of the worst business responses to sudden turbulence and recession is to institute across-the-board cost cuts where, for example, every department must cut its costs by 10 percent. Imagine a highly regarded service company having to cut its service budget by 10 percent (better trim the fat, not the service!). Imagine advertising being cut by 10 percent at a time when the company needs more, not less advertising, albeit spent in a different way.

Some CEOs ask each branch office and subsidiary to cut expenses by a certain percentage, but they ask each branch manager to decide on what gets cut. This is wise because each branch faces different threats and opportunities.

Within the marketing arena, those in charge at the onset of a recession are advised to consider the following possible moves straight out of the traditional two-playbook strategy planning guide—one for up-markets, the other for down-markets:

- Drop losing customer segments.

- Drop losing customers within a segment.

- Drop losing geographical locations.

- Drop losing products.

- Lower prices or promote lower-cost brands.

- Reduce or discontinue ads and promotions that aren't working.

Consider how Procter & Gamble decided to cut marketing costs from 25 percent to 20 percent of sales to remain competitive in a down-market. The company:

- Standardized more product formulations, packaging, and advertising around the world

- Reduced the number of sizes and flavors of products offered

- Dropped or sold some weaker brands

- Launched fewer but more promising brands

- Reduced trade and consumer promotions

- Reduced the rate of advertising growth

The P&G example indicates that every company must search carefully for ways to reduce marketing costs when facing deteriorating market situations. Here is a checklist of questions you should start asking. Can your company:

- Lower the costs of paper, photography, and other production inputs by negotiating for lower prices or switching to lower-cost suppliers?

- Switch to lower-cost transportation carriers?

- Close down sales offices if they are not getting enough use? (Field sales personnel can work out of their homes instead of traveling to an office.)

- Put your advertising agency on a pay-for-performance compensation plan instead of offering a standard commission regardless of the results?

- Replace higher-cost communication channels with lower-cost channels? (E-mail is cheaper than direct mail.)

- Achieve more impact by shifting money for thirty-second commercials into public relations or new digital media?

- Drop some product features or services for which customers don't seem to care?

- Hold your marketing staff meetings and customer conferences in lower-cost locations?

These troubled economic times are forcing all marketing executives to reevaluate their spending plans. Addressing the following five tough questions will help leaders determine how best to reduce and reallocate their budgets:[1]

1. *Do you have a complete inventory of your growth investments and can you identify waste (or inefficient spend)?* Periodically taking an investment inventory will reveal wasteful spending of as much as 15 percent almost every time, along with proven winners that must be supported no matter how much the budget must be reduced. A thorough inventory identifies obvious wastes and clear producers, as well as spending areas that pose bottom-line opportunities for more efficient and effective spending.

2. *Do your investments change your customers' buying behavior?* Share of market and revenue goals are too general to be true barometers of effectiveness. It is more important to know what specific behaviors you are trying to drive among specific segments of customers. For one customer segment, it may be driving an annual versus biannual service package upgrade; for another, it may be to motivate customers to buy 50 percent more each time they order. By identifying growth-generating behaviors, you can judge your marketing investments by their ability to drive those behaviors.

3. *Are your investments focused on customers' barriers to buying your brand?* Try to understand the barriers to buying and then choose the marketing vehicles and messages that will overcome these barriers. For example, one high market share company spent heavily on mass advertising to build awareness—which is efficient if you are examining the cost divided by the number of prospects.

But the brand was already well known. A better course would be to spend money on closing the sale—a shift that actually could significantly increase growth. Conversely, a low market share company first needs to bump up awareness to higher levels, in which case mass advertising works best.

4. *Do you have the right mix of marketing levers among your investments?* All marketing investments do at least one of three things: (1) change customer perceptions to encourage them to buy more, (2) provide temporary monetary incentives for customers to buy more, or (3) make the brand more available so customers can buy more. Focusing too heavily on any one lever can hurt the others. Instead, thinking must shift to weigh the right mix of investments and generate profitable growth.

5. *Do you have a system to maintain "winners" and cut "losers?"* As you assess your winning and losing investments, it is critical to think about both the potential long-term and short-term impacts of those decisions. Four considerations should guide this evaluation: (1) effectiveness and efficiency, (2) maintenance versus growth, (3) proven versus experimental, and (4) direct and indirect impact.

Knowing which marketing strategies to deploy during periods of economic downturn is challenging. Yet such times also provide new opportunities. Assessing and aligning your marketing activities with these five critical questions will enable greater effectiveness, efficiency, and returns—regardless of the economy.

Strategic Marketing Responses to Crises

The main thing to remember during periods of turbulence is that your customers are likely to change; therefore you have to change. If you know where your customers are moving, you have to be ready to adjust your offerings. It is not enough to cut your costs. You must adjust your product line and service package.

Let's consider this task in relation to what restaurants should do when facing soaring food costs and the fact that consumers drive less when fuel costs rise. Customers are on a tighter budget. Many customers will switch to cheaper restaurants or to cheaper dishes at the same restaurants. One of the first things consumers do is order fewer appetizers and desserts. In that case, what options do restaurants have to cut expenses yet keep customers and make a profit? They generally choose one or more of four responses:

- *Cut the portion size.* Americans are used to oversize servings. Now is the time to trim the size and reduce the cost. The TGI Friday restaurant chain chose during the 2008 recession to offer slimmed-down portion sizes.

- *Lower the price.* The restaurant can lower its prices on one or more items. The Outback restaurant chain advertised a steak meal for under $10.00 that consisted of a six-ounce sirloin with salad, baked potato, and bread for $9.99. The Hooters restaurant chain reduced its draft beer price to $1.00.

- *Maintain the same price, but add something.* The Friendly's restaurant chain still charges $9.99 for an entrée, but now it comes with a two-scoop ice cream sundae. The Denny's restaurant chain offers an "Express Slam" with two eggs, two pancakes, two bacon strips, and two sausage links for $4.00 from 5 a.m. to 4 p.m. daily.

- *Lower the quality of food and ingredients.* Some restaurants substitute flank steak for sirloin steak or lower-quality chicken for higher quality, or they may use less butter or even substitute margarine in their cooking. This approach to cutting expenses carries a risk that the customers will be disappointed and not return.

Clearly, every company that's trying to appeal to more budget-constrained customers has to list its alternatives and think hard about the implication of each move it makes. Customers have certain expectations and experiences, so the company has to decide on the best strategy mix that will keep its customers coming. The company must choose steps that will preserve its value proposition and appeal while lowering its costs.

A company must also choose its strategy mix in relation to what its competitors are doing (or may do). Suppose your competitors have been cutting their prices. This leaves you with little choice but to cut your prices or add some strong benefits. Or suppose your competitors have not cut their prices. Should your company stand still or be the first to lower prices, knowing that some competitors will be forced to retaliate by cutting *their* prices?

Companies must also try to think positively about opportunities that may be created by the turbulence. Some companies see crises as opportunity. A prominent banker once commented that his bank cannot do much to improve its market share during normal times. But when lightning strikes and some of his competitors are weakened, he can acquire them inexpensively, or he can win market share more easily—provided that he has cash and is willing to take some risk.

Marketers will face many new challenges in the foreseeable future with sporadic turbulence continuing in the environment. During past swings in the economy—as well as during full-blown recessions—experienced marketers learned how to keep business moving forward. Once through the recessions of the past, marketers returned to their "upturn-oriented" marketing plans with the assurance that, once safely through the recession, they had at least a good six or seven years before the next downturn. Not so any longer.

Marketing plans in The Age of Turbulence need to ramp up quickly and show resilience. One of the biggest challenges for marketers will be keeping the cost-cutting wolves at bay to minimally maintain their pre-recession budgets and, even better, to have them increased. The pressure on marketers to justify marketing expenditures may likely increase to levels never before experienced.

Marketers should be aware of the growing likelihood of deflation for two reasons. First, there is no need to get locked into long-term commitments on advertising time and space because ad rates will be among the first targets of discounting when times get tough. Add deflation to the mix and media/advertising rates will likely drop a lot. Second, marketing strategies will need to be honed to appeal to increasingly skittish customers who will be in no hurry to buy your products (or anyone else's) this month when next month's prices may be lower.

The signs of turbulence are all over, and they are not going away anytime soon. In fact, marketers need to develop a new mindset of always being on hot standby to activate automatic response marketing programs when the turbulence whips up and chaos reigns. In doing so, marketers need to keep in mind the following eight factors as they create their chaotics marketing strategies:

1. *Secure your market share from core customer segments.* This is no time to get too greedy, so be sure your first priority is to get your core customer segments firmly secured, and be prepared to ward off attacks from competitors attempting to take away your most profitable and loyal customers.

2. *Push aggressively for greater market share from competitors matching up to your core customer segments.* All companies fight for market share and, in turbulent and chaotic times, many have been weakened. Slashing marketing budgets and sales travel expenses is a sure sign that a competitor is buckling under pressure. Push aggressively to add to your core customer segments at the expense of your weakened competitors.

3. *Research customers more now because their needs and wants are in flux.* Everyone is under pressure during times of turbulence and chaos, which means all customers are changing their habits—even those customers in your core segments whom you know so well. Stay close to them. Research them more now than ever before. You don't want to find yourself relying on old "tried-and-true" marketing messages that no longer resonate.

4. *Seek to increase—or at least maintain—your marketing budget.* With the market being buffeted by turbulence and your customers getting whipsawed by it (and aggressively marketed to by your competitors), this is the worst time to even think about cutting anything in your marketing budget that targets your core customer segments. In fact, you need to add to this budget, or take money away from those forays you were planning to go after totally new customer segments. It's time to secure the home front.

5. *Focus on all that's safe and emphasize core values.* When turbulence is scaring everyone in the market, there is a massive flight to safety by most consumers. This is the time when they need to feel the safety and security of your company and your products and services. Do everything possible to communicate that continuing to do business with you is safe. Sell customers products and services that continue to make them feel safe—and spend whatever it takes to do it.

6. *Quickly drop programs that aren't working for you.* Your marketing budgets will always be scrutinized, in good times as well as bad times. Cut out any ineffective program you know of before someone else calls attention to it. If you are not watching your spending, rest assured that someone else is, including all your peers whose budgets couldn't be protected from the ax.

7. *Don't discount your best brands.* Everyone tells you not to discount your established and most successful brands for good reason. When you discount them, you instantly tell the market two things: Your prices were too high before you discounted them, and they won't be worth the price in the future once the discounts are gone. If you want to appeal to more frugal customer needs and wants, then create a new, separate, and distinct product or service offering under a new brand with lower prices. This gives value-conscious customers the ability to stay close to you, while not alienating those who still are willing to pay for your higher-priced brands. Once the turbulence subsides and you see some calm skies ahead, you may consider discontinuing your newly introduced branded value product line—or maybe not. Remember, it is better for you to cannibalize your products than for your competitors to do so; at least you have the ability to upsell them to customers— if they are still your customers.

8. *Save the strong; lose the weak:* In turbulent markets, you need to make your strongest brands and products even stronger. There's no time or money to be wasted on marginal brands or overly fragile products that are not supported by strong value propositions and a solid customer base. Tie in the need to appeal to safety and value to reinforce already strong brands and strong service or product offerings. Remember, your brands can never be strong enough, especially against the strong waves of a turbulent economy.

When marketing executives see that the economy or their industry is in for a rough period, which in the new environment will often last for several months or even a few years at a time, they can now look to a concise checklist of strategic behaviors, developed solely for marketing, to guide them. As shown in Figure 5–1, the necessary actions to take are: Cut/Delay, Outsource, Increase/Accelerate.

CUT / DELAY	OUTSOURCE	INCREASE / ACCELERATE
■ Marketing programs that are not working	■ Marketing support services	■ Marketing budgets overall
■ Advertising programs that are not working	■ Promotions support services	■ Market research budget
■ Weak products and services		■ Price research budget
■ Noncore product and service introductions, unless highly innovative		■ Advertising budget
■ Plans to discount core brands		■ Promotions budget
■ Noncore advertising and promotions		■ Focus on core segments
		■ New market share gains in core segments
		■ Development of new, separately branded products and services for value-conscious customers
		■ Alignment of value-to-price propositions
		■ Customer loyalty programs
		■ New product introductions of high innovation products and services
		■ Key account customized marketing communications
		■ Distribution partner channel marketing communications
		■ Stakeholder marketing communications

Figure 5-1. Chaotics strategic behavior checklist for marketing.

Operational Issues Facing the Marketing Department

The marketing department is typically headed by a marketing director, a marketing vice president, or a chief marketing officer (CMO). When ordered to cut the marketing budget because of a slowdown, these executives may initially argue that they need the present budget if they are to prop up sales. If they cut the budget, sales will fall faster. But the burden is on them to convince the CEO and CFO that planned marketing expenditures are necessary to preserve sales or at least slow the decline. They will probably lose the battle.

That leaves them considering what to cut from the various marketing activities.

MARKETING RESEARCH

Clearly, marketing executives will want to do some market research to understand how customers are changing. Otherwise they will have to depend solely on their own intuition and/or salespeople's views and experiences. They may decide, however, to cancel a few planned marketing research studies that would have delivered useful results in normal times. They will probably cancel any large-scale attitude survey that takes a few months to complete and report. There's no time, these studies are too expensive, and the findings may prove to be less relevant during a turbulent period than normal times.

PRODUCTS

This is a time to reexamine the whole product line. Hopefully, every product line consists of today's hot winners and yesterday's faithful standbys, as well as some old dogs. The slower-selling items are tolerated in normal times. But the times are not normal. This may finally force some difficult decisions on which products to clear out of the line because they have little promise of generating profits.

Many good-selling products are full-featured and capable of offering more functionality than customers will use. This is true of computers, cameras, and other equipment. Companies are proud to offer the latest in technology. But this may be the right time to produce a simpler model with limited functionality to appeal to buyers who want a product at a lower price: the computer that only does word processing, or the mobile phone, with which you can do only that—phone—for example.

NEW PRODUCT INTRODUCTIONS

Every company knows that the choice is between innovation and stagnation. If you don't innovate, you will stagnate. That explains the new product lineup that you have prepared to launch in normal times. But the times aren't normal. Some of the new products have to be put on the back burner. The world may not need a different size or flavor of product at this time. But there may be a few new and promising product ideas. Some may address the customer's search for a lower price or higher value. Those new products can be kept on the front burner since they may address the very problem that your customers are facing.

SERVICE

Companies usually offer a bundle of services that go with different levels of buying. A hospital that buys an MRI machine from General Electric will get installation, training, maintenance and repair service, and upgrades as part of the purchase plan. A university will offer students a dormitory plan, a food service plan, a health plan, and study and entertainment facilities.

Nevertheless, a company needs to distinguish between services that are essential to the product purchase and services that are more discretionary. The latter might not be packaged with the purchase of the product, but may be made available for separate purchase. The company will make money on some of these discretionary services and lose money on others. The profitability and necessity of the different services should be evaluated. One area of potential cost savings: unnecessary services that cost more than they are worth to buyers.

ADVERTISING

If the company spends heavily on thirty-second TV commercials, these buys will have to be cut down or eliminated. This is the easiest way to save a lot of money. The marketing head usually cannot provide hard evidence as to their effectiveness, anyway. If the company's ads don't carry any new information relevant to customers' situations during a recession, they must be canceled. If Coca-Cola hasn't found a way to say something new and relevant, its advertising doesn't do much good.

The marketing head has to rethink the company's expenditures on other media as well, such as newspapers, magazines, radio, and billboards. He and the advertising agency account executive have to reexamine the relative strengths of the company's brand in different geographical markets. There are always some cities and regions where the company's brand is weak compared to competitors. Expenditures on newspapers and radio stations in weak markets should be cut. The money is better used to defend and expand the company's market share in those markets where it is strong. These are tough decisions, and they won't make the salespeople in the weaker markets happy.

The real need is to move some of the funds to new digital media, which are often less costly. For example, if the company has been sending out direct-mail offers and catalogs, it may want to consider using e-mail or web-based catalogs rather than paper-based mailings. The company may find it helpful to run a webinar explaining to customers how they can save money during the downturn. Smart companies will try to help their customers sail through the turbulent waters. They may prepare and distribute one or more fifteen-minute podcasts that customers can download to get help in buying or operating products. The company should operate one or more blogs providing useful information to customers. And it should consider ways to use the social networking sites such as Facebook to send relevant messages to specific customers.

PRICING

No doubt companies will find themselves under strong pressure to cut prices, especially if this is the route that their competitors are taking. It is almost always better not to cut prices, but to offer some additional benefits instead, such as paying for the freight or offering a longer guarantee on the product. But these tactics may not work. This leaves two price-cutting possibilities: One is to present some stripped-down versions of the company's offerings at a lower price. For example, a printer may normally carry a year of free repair service. Now the company can offer the product for less, but with only a thirty-day period of free repairs. The other approach is to offer a sales price, discount, or rebate on current products. We know that department stores clear their merchandise by offering a succession of deep and deeper discounts. Auto companies advertise sales or rebates when they want to move cars. While price cuts usually work, the problem is that they can damage the brand image. If a company's products are on sale 30 percent or more of the time, people start to think of the original price as being phony and not reflecting the quality of the brand.

MARGINS

When it comes to striking a balance between sales volume and profit margins in turbulent markets, it takes an experienced marketer to navigate through the rough waters. Here are three important recommendations for keeping your margins above water while you are pushing for deeper market share:

▪ *Price and value proposition adjustments must keep up with changing customer needs.* Turbulent times always trigger changes in customer needs and wants, and in the value propositions that appeal most to them when they are feeling unsure about their situations— even with their long-established suppliers. During times of extreme turbulence and chaos, these changes in customer preferences can happen much more rapidly. In such difficult environments, the best companies are keeping a close pulse on the changing economics of their customers. When they see shifting preferences and patterns developing, they quickly react by reconfiguring their pricing and value propositions to meet those changes.

▪ *Keep a steady lookout for sudden changes in pricing structures.* When tough times hit, so too does desperation for many of your customers, as well as for many of your competitors. When their desperation grows high enough, it may be manifested by sudden changes in pricing policies and/or pricing preferences—typically leading to falling prices and discounts. This creates an ideal environment for unsuspecting suppliers to get caught in a tight margin squeeze. Companies need to be increasingly alert in monitoring pricing policies that reduce revenue (e.g., volume discounts, rebates, and cash discounts) as well as those policies that increase the costs to serve (e.g., shipping and transportation, technical or customer support). Companies must review their margins on a per-customer basis more frequently to maintain respectable margins from every possible customer. Without the extra attention and quick action, margin erosion at any of the points in the sales and fulfillment cycles can quickly erode profits during turbulent times.

▪ *Continually update price sensitivity data.* Whenever there are wide swings in raw material, commodity, or energy prices, there is a direct impact on the pricing of virtually all downstream goods and services. Such dramatic price increases make customers and consumers much more sensitive to prices. To get pricing right during turbulent times, more time and effort must be devoted to conducting continuous pricing-sensitivity research, along with price tests in the market, with rapid-response scenarios already constructed to get pricing quickly back on track to keep current with the changes in the market.

DISTRIBUTION

Many companies operate through middlemen who carry and sell the company's product to their own customers. These middlemen are wholesalers, jobbers, dealers, retailers, manufacturers' agents, and so on. A company chooses these middlemen carefully and also audits their results. Usually some middlemen do exceptionally well; at the other extreme are middlemen who barely cover the cost of using them. Weaker middlemen are usually terminated in normal times, but a slowdown doesn't seem to be a time when the company wants to trim them and suffer even lower sales.

The real effort is to go all out in helping and motivating these third parties to push the company's products. The sales force needs to show them how profitable it is for them to carry the company's products and even to give them more shelf space. For example, the marketing department could prepare more displays, promotions, and incentives that the sales representatives can use to generate more enthusiasm and a bigger push from their third-party agents.

Operational Issues Facing the Sales Department

It is pretty difficult to conduct "business as usual" when economic news is anything but usual. With the threat of tougher economic times, new prospects have all but disappeared, existing customers are tightening their budgets for the coming months, and most of the "low-hanging fruit" has already been picked, packaged, and eaten. Economic conditions have definitely changed—so where does that leave your sales organization?

The natural tendency for salespeople—and maybe senior executives, too—is to panic. With the bottom line looking as though it is in jeopardy, companies are scrambling to reduce headcount and cut back on expenses. Meanwhile, top executives are looking for ways to boost revenue, which usually means turning up the heat on the sales organization to produce more sales.

Before sales executives lose heart, they need to begin to look for hidden opportunities during difficult economic times. And they need to communicate these newfound opportunities to their sales teams.

First, find the strong and weak points in your sales team, which can become an exercise to strengthen the entire sales operation, making it even more competitive as times begin to improve.

Second, tough economic times provide the opportunity to do the things that should have been done in the first place, including dropping marginally successful sales promotions or letting go of non-performing salespeople who have already had enough chances to improve their sales during good times.

Third, downturns in the economy absolutely create new sales opportunities because so much is changing. Customers are looking for new, more appropriate value propositions keyed into the difficult times. And that does not always mean discounting prices. They need to do more with less, and your salespeople need to help them do it. Marketing and sales must tighten up their communications with each other to determine the new value propositions that customers need.

Increasing the pressure on the sales team doesn't necessarily translate into increased revenue. Sales managers can help their sales forces bring in a few short-term deals, but at the end of the day, customers don't respond well when they feel pressured into buying. Here, then, are six key steps for sales executives to get their sales teams to take on the tough economy and increase those badly needed sales:

1. *Think high touch.* Get back to basic selling strategies during down times. Salespeople need to get even closer to their customers, and that means seeing people face-to-face. As tempting as it is to cut back on travel, sales during difficult economic times can't be done with much success by e-mail or the phone.

2. *Build team spirit.* To keep up morale, keep the communication channels open. Sales executives need to understand what's going on with their teams, so they've got to turn up the two-way communications with sales managers and salespeople alike. Top sales executives need to understand their people and their people need to understand them. Communicate more personally with them. Listen to their problems, and turn their problems into opportunities to motivate them.

3. *Don't cave in to pressure to do any deals.* The problem with discounting to stay in business and make a smaller profit is that when good times return, it will be hard to get prices back up to where they need to be. More important, you send the wrong signals to your salespeople and you confuse them. Once sales executives open the door and allow their sales teams to discount, the sales teams will resist letting that door close again.

4. *Find new ways to get sales teams motivated.* Keeping up morale takes constant effort, and it's worth it. Something as simple as a twenty-minute pep talk with the sales teams can make a big difference, boosting their morale and their sales results. Also, develop a variety of incentive-building contests, some of which allow salespeople to compete individually and others where they compete in teams.

5. *Keep expectations high, but not impossible.* Sales executives must guard against setting sights too low or too high. In an effort to avoid demanding the impossible, sales executives can actually demotivate people by lowering their expectations too much.

6. *Protect the sales teams' base salaries.* Don't change base salaries when times get tough; protect them. And be reasonable about goals, objectives, and quotas for sales managers and their teams. Set them more realistically in line with market conditions and with a greater knowledge of the specific realities of customer segments and accounts.

The sales force is often one of the largest costs, especially in business-to-business companies and where the products being sold are complex, such as heavy equipment. Companies normally set variable-pay elements in the remuneration scheme, such as commissions, incentives, and bonuses that in some cases may add up to 50 percent to 70 percent of the pay received. This policy protects the company against down-market developments because the sales force shares some of the risk. But in those companies where most remuneration for salespeople is fixed, there is a greater urgency to introduce staffing cuts. In every sales force there is a disproportion between the performance of the best salespeople and the worst. The worst are tolerated during normal or prosperous periods because their below-normal level of sales still adds net profit. But in turbulent times, where most remuneration is a fixed expense to the company, staff cuts are much more warranted.

The company has to consider a larger number of issues related to the role of the sales force and their targets. Here are a few of the many questions that arise in trying to repattern sales force activity to be profitable and productive during a downdraft period:

CUT / DELAY	OUTSOURCE	INCREASE / ACCELERATE
■ Head count increases ■ Trade shows and other activities that are not directly related to a sale ■ Fixed compensation	■ Sales to noncore and small accounts ■ Lead generation sources ■ Customer service to noncore accounts ■ Service/repair calls ■ Warranty support ■ Noncore business development activities	■ Knowledge of, and agreements with, all key distribution channel partners ■ New channel development ■ Competitive intelligence ■ Customer loyalty promotions ■ Strategic alliances with firms selling to same target market ■ Cross-selling, up-selling ■ Accuracy of sales forecasts ■ Customer contacts (meetings, communications) ■ Sales team contacts and communications ■ Sales skills, negotiations skills, product and soft skills training

Figure 5-2. Chaotics strategic behaviors checklist for sales.

∎ Should the company close some sales offices or territories here and abroad, in locations where current and future sales are very marginal?

∎ Should sales managers be assigned to manage a larger number of salespeople than normal, as a way to spread the costs of sales management, hopefully without lowering the quality of sales management and control?

∎ Should sales targets remain at the same level or be reduced, to recognize the downturn and allow salespeople to believe the targets and the pay for performance are reasonable?

∎ Should training programs be dropped to save money or increased to give the salespeople new ideas and tools for selling to reluctant customers?

When sales executives are asked what their groups can do to help their firms increase sales, they can now look to a checklist of strategic behaviors, developed expressly for their departments. The checklist, shown in Figure 5–2, outlines the necessary actions to take.

Conclusion

We have shown that turbulent times call for many changes—both strategic and tactical—in a company's marketing efforts. The worst thing is to just enforce a large across-the-board cut in the marketing budget. The marketing head may try to defend keeping the existing budget, primarily as the best way to shore up sales, but she may not be able to convince the CEO and CFO. In fact, they will likely push cuts in the advertising budget, particularly the high expenditures associated with thirty-second commercials.

From a strategic point of view, companies must remain focused on satisfying their target customers, paying particular attention to their best customers. In many businesses, a small percentage of customers account for a disproportionate percentage of sales.

Companies cannot start to make cost cuts until they grasp what is happening to their customers, competitors, dealers, and suppliers. What problems face their customers? What moves are those customers making? How can the company provide help to their customers? What are the competitors doing? What opportunities are opening up in the meantime? How much risk does the company want to take? Each company must act in a way that best promises to preserve its customers, its brand strength, and its long-term objectives.

We reviewed the main marketing activities that would call for a review and possible cost savings, such as marketing research, product mix, services, advertising, pricing, and distribution. All of these activities interact, and therefore any cut in one area is likely to set up reverberations in the other areas. Clearly, the company needs to develop a vision of what strategic and tactical responses are available during a slowdown—and in particular during a long, extended slowdown. And finally, the company must develop a sense of the possible scenarios and work out a view of appropriate responses to address each scenario.

CHAPTER SIX

Thriving in The Age of Turbulence

Achieving Business Enterprise Sustainability

A defender must always seek to change over to the attack; as soon as he has gained the benefit of the defense.
> —Carl Phillip Gottfried von Clausewitz, On War[1]

BUSINESS IS NOT warfare, contrary to what became a popular business theme and book genre in the 1990s. In the business world today, a competitor may also be one of your customers, suppliers, distributors, or investors. One entity may play many roles. So, *destroying* a competitor could mean harming oneself.

It may seem odd that we begin the discussion of Business Enterprise Sustainability with a quote from one of history's most brilliant military strategists, Carl von Clausewitz, the great Prussian soldier and intellectual from the early-nineteenth century. We do so not to provide specific military strategies or tactics to apply in today's turbulent world; rather, we raise three underlying principles of strategy execution amidst chaos, both in business and in battle: (1) Disorientation and confusion reign; (2) communication is imperative; and (3) achieving the ultimate objective guides all actions. It is these three principles that will guide our discussion in this final chapter of *Chaotics.* Our ultimate objective is to provide a guide for business leaders to create businesses that will live on and thrive despite the turbulence and chaos they may encounter.

In conversations with top business leaders about operating profitably in periods of high uncertainty and turbulence, three questions seem to be foremost on their minds:

- In an environment where raw material and other key costs in business jump up 25 percent, 50 percent, 100 percent, or more (or dive downward by these same amounts) in just a matter of months, how can we react more quickly, especially when it takes at least three months to get even small adjustments to drive strategy through the organization?

- In an environment where businesses have increasingly less control in overcoming dramatic, unpredictable disruptions, how, when we just passed through one storm and another is brewing, do we gain a firmer control of the rudder to steer the organization through to calmer waters?

- In an environment where the more successful we become, the larger our companies also become (which creates even greater problems as we react to the turbulence swirling around us), how do we overcome the paradox of such growth systematically retarding our organizations' reaction time?

One business executive summarized these three questions in a single statement: "We've got costs rising dramatically—and also some dropping just as dramatically—within incredibly short time cycles. That requires a faster reaction time than most businesses can handle. It's akin to asking me to turn ninety degrees in an instant, which is possible when driving a jet ski over even the most turbulent waters, but virtually impossible when piloting a massive ocean freighter even in the calmest of seas, which is precisely what it's like heading up a multibillion-dollar global organization."

To answer these three questions, we need to merge the new insights presented in the preceding chapters with pragmatic steps that business executives can take. Here are three specific actions:

1. Make strategic planning more dynamic, interactive, and compressed into shorter time cycles—sequenced in three-month intervals, rather than reviewed and adjusted once a year. In these shorter cycles, responsibilities, authorities, accountabilities, and performance measurements may be realigned as needed.

2. Facilitate cross-functional decision making at key levels to drive better, faster decisions. Key decision makers must be in closer physical proximity and connected with more frequent and faster interactive communication channels. More stakeholder representatives should be included in the discussion and decision-making process.

3. Break large organizations down into smaller, flatter groups and subgroups to facilitate and achieve faster reaction times. Responsibilities, authorities, and accountabilities should be driven down to the lowest possible level. Hard and soft skills must be raised significantly to improve the quality of decisions. The smaller groups must be able to reach other relevant groups on a global basis.

Business Enterprise Sustainability (BES)

Business Enterprise Sustainability (BES) is essentially focused on *all* issues integral to extending the life of the business enterprise for as long as possible. It is recognition of the social, economic, environmental, and ethical factors that directly affect business strategy. These factors include how companies attract and retain employees and how they manage the risks and create opportunities from climate change, a company's culture, corporate-governance standards, stakeholder-engagement strategies, philanthropy, reputation, and brand management. Today, these factors are particularly important given the widening of societal expectations of corporate responsibility.[2]

Business enterprise sustainability aims for a comprehensive strategy to maximize the underlying value of companies in the extended long term, while optimizing company performance and value in the short and medium term—but never to compromise long-term value. It involves a number of components, including a responsive, robust, and resilient business strategy at its core. Critical to such a strategy are the preservation of well-maintained assets, ongoing replenishment of innovative products and services, and a favorable reputation with customers, employees, distributors and suppliers, governments, and other key stakeholders investing in the business.

Too often, business leaders confuse high growth with high performance. They may take unwise risks in their businesses to maximize short- or medium-term profitability, while at the same time jeopardizing the company's long-term viability. They may destroy long-term value through their overly ambitious growth plans, which sometimes include unwise and expensive acquisitions to increase shareholder value in the short term.

Certainly growth is important to the sustainability of any business, but longer-term sustainability should override any short-term or even medium-term ambitions—especially in turbulent and unpredictable environments where chaos, if not managed well, could cause irreparable harm and even sink a business permanently.

Here we will describe some of the characteristics of those companies that have achieved Business Enterprise Sustainability in the long term. Let's begin with how such successful companies "view" their planning horizon and what goes into that planning.

DUAL VISION

We have examined how companies can survive and prosper in a global world characterized by an accelerating rate of change and increasing turbulence. We have tried to show how companies that operate primarily to do well in the short term are likely to incur problems in the long run. For example, requiring an across-the-board cut in everyone's budget saves money in the short run, but is likely to weaken the company's position in the long run. Why? Because projects are put on hold, marketing research is reduced or canceled, advertising (the company's ability to make an impression) is severely reduced, and some talented employees are dismissed. GM and Ford, for example, introduced no down payments and employee discounts to stimulate short-term demand. It worked. Sales went up by 40 percent. Three months later sales plummeted. They borrowed from the future.

We would argue that companies need to operate with one eye focused on the short term and the other eye focused on the long term. We call this managing with "dual vision." The need is to balance both visions in normal as well as in turbulent periods:

Planning for Today

- Clearly defining the business
- Shaping the business to meet the needs of todays customers
- Improving alignment between functional activities and business definition

- Mirroring current business activities

- Optimizing current operations to achieve excellence

Planning for tomorrow

- Redefining the business

- Reshaping the business to compete for future customers and markets

- Making bold moves away from the existing ways of doing business

- Reorganizing for future business challenges

- Managing change to create future operations and processes[3]

A focus on *today* shapes the business to meet the needs of today's customers—and it does so with excellence and authenticity. It seeks to maximize the business's effectiveness in its functional activities that mirrors current business opportunities.

A focus on *tomorrow* projects a reshaping of the business to compete more effectively in the future. Often, this demands bold moves away from the present to reorganize and reshape for future challenges.

Business leaders who understand dual vision also realize that in doing business in the age of turbulence, one of the tremendous challenges is to plan and manage the current model while fending off chaos, and simultaneously visioning the future, forging the plans for tomorrow, and managing the change process to effect that vision.

TRIPLE PLANNING

We would also argue that companies need to work at three planning levels: short term, intermediate term (three to five years), and long term. Professor Vijay Govindarajan at Dartmouth[4] says that every company in normal times should put its projects and initiatives in three boxes: short term, mid-term, and long term.

SHORT TERM

The short-term box is about *managing the present.* It should include projects related to improving the core business. Most of the projects have to do with filling the *performance gap* in the core business. It may be striving to reach Six Sigma performance; it may be rightsizing or copying the best practices of competitors. Most of these projects are operational and aimed at gaining more efficiency.

MID-TERM

The mid-term box is about *selectively forgetting the past.* It should include projects aimed at entering adjacent spaces next to the core business. These projects are not about performance improvement as much as filling the *opportunity gap.* The company needs to exploit nonlinear, discontinuous changes such as the Internet, new media, customer empowerment, and the rise of emerging countries such as China and India.

LONG TERM

The long-term box is *entirely new space.* It should include concepts for the future—say, for the year 2020—that may or may not be possible. Examples: going to the moon, unraveling the human genome, a $2,000 car, a $100 computer, and other dream projects. Projects of this kind are characterized by a high ratio of assumptions to knowledge. But by working slowly on these concepts and learning more, the ratio of assumptions to knowledge will fall over time.

In normal times, a company may put 50 percent of its projects in box 1, 30 percent in box 2, and 20 percent in box 3. If it doesn't have a project in box 3, it isn't a challenged company with a dream of bringing some big new ideas to life!

When turbulence strikes, many companies are likely to change these ratios. A *panicked company* will work only on box 1 and even then may drop several short-term projects. A *calmer company* would continue a few of its box 2 (mid-term) projects and probably put no time into box 3 (long-term dream projects). A *smart company* would probably keep projects in all three boxes, although reducing the number. The point is, the calmer and smarter companies, and in particular the smart companies, have the best chance of not only surviving in the present but also emerging with a long and strong future.

All said, a company would be wise to manage in three planning horizons. Its employees will be especially motivated by the dream in the third box, but they will also be motivated by the challenges in the second box. And this will be true of the other stakeholders— suppliers, distributors, investors—who have a special interest in and feeling for this type of company.

COMPANY REPUTATION

In any given industry, the reputations of the main contenders will vary greatly. Consider the auto industry in the United States. At one time, the most prized automobile companies in the U.S. marketplace were General Motors, Ford, and Chrysler ("the Big Three"). Americans could buy a car from these companies with some confidence, but they and their European counterparts would have a little less confidence in any upstart U.S. or European auto producers and even less in some of the new Chinese automobile manufacturers such as Chery, Geely, or Shanghai Automotive Industry Corporation. Company size had a lot to do with reputation, but there were other factors as well. China's small but ambitious automobile companies are not well known in the United States, Europe, or other parts of the world outside of China, but could one day become household names, just like Toyota, Honda, and Nissan.

"Chinese automakers are all still establishing themselves in terms of products, quality, and manufacturing—the very things that go into running a successful automotive company," said Tim Dunne, director for Asia Pacific market intelligence at J. D. Power and Associates.[5] And it will take time—a lot of time—for the new Chinese automakers, and all aspiring companies seeking to become great companies, to establish solid reputations.

Today, the best reputations in the U.S. auto market belong not to the Big Three, but rather to companies such as Toyota, Honda, Mercedes, BMW, and a few others. There are many reasons for the reversal in reputation. For one thing, the companies with good reputations today deliver to the public more auto reliability, more innovation, and better service. In fact, most people today would bet that Toyota, Honda, and Nissan will be around much longer than General Motors, Ford, or Chrysler, unless the latter companies can radically improve their reputations through innovation and customer care.

What goes into a company's reputation? What factors must a company manage to be viewed favorably by its stakeholders in good times as well as in turbulent times?

Since 1999, Harris Interactive, Inc. has been conducting an annual study that ranks the reputations of America's corporations as viewed by the American public. In 2008, the Harris Interactive Corporate Reputation study found that 71 percent of Americans believe the reputation of Corporate America is "poor," but some companies are bucking the trend and building positive, public brand reputations.[6]

At the top of the Harris Interactive list of the sixty most visible companies in the U.S. with a positive reputation is Google, which kicked Microsoft out of the top spot in 2008. Microsoft held the number-one spot for just one year after ousting Johnson & Johnson, which had held it since the study began nine years ago. Check out the top-ten Corporate America Reputations for 2008, according to Harris Interactive. In descending order:

1. Google

2. Johnson & Johnson

3. Intel Corporation

4. General Mills

5. Kraft Foods Inc.

6. Berkshire Hathaway Inc.

7. 3M Company

8. The Coca-Cola Company

9. Honda Motor Co.

10. Microsoft Corporation

Harris Interactive uses six specific factors to determine ratings of company reputations that they survey each year, which include: (1) Emotional Appeal, (2) Products and Services, (3) Workplace Environment, (4) Financial Performance, (5) Vision and Leadership, and (6) Social Responsibility.

While all six factors are key, some are clearly more important than others. We suggest that the most important factor is the customers' and stakeholders' perception of the company's *Products and Services.* Are they of high quality? Are they innovative? Do they give good value for the money, and are they backed by excellent service? If these attributes are missing, the other factors can't compensate.

A reputation for social responsibility cannot make up for producing and delivering poor products and services. Even if the company's financial performance is strong, it won't be strong for long if unhappy consumers broadcast their disappointment to other consumers over the Internet and in person.

The second most important factor is *Vision and Leadership.* Stakeholders like to see evidence of a clear company vision about what the company will be good at and where it is going. And if the top management team is well respected and dynamic, this adds even more confidence in the firm.

The third factor in order of importance is the *Workplace Environment,* because it shows how well the company treats its employees and how satisfied employees are with their opportunities and treatment. Every year, *Fortune* magazine ranks the 100 best places to work in the United States.[7] We know that companies with a strong reputation for employee satisfaction can recruit the best, most productive employees. We also know that dissatisfied employees have an increasing number of Internet tools available to broadcast their low opinions of a company and its poor treatment of employees.

The fourth most important factor is the company's *Financial Performance* relative both to its competitors and its expected profits over time in relation to the level of risk. An additional issue is whether the firm shows healthy growth as well as profitability.

The fifth factor, *Emotional Appeal,* represents how customers and other stakeholders feel about the company, whether they like it and trust it. Clearly, customers can have different feelings about a set of competitors with similar offerings and operations. Consider the decades-long, high level of emotional attachment customers feel toward such companies as Harley-Davidson, LEGO, Apple, Nike, and Starbucks.

The sixth factor is the company's *Social Responsibility.* This factor has grown in importance in recent years. Customers are more attracted to companies that seem to care about societal issues such as poverty, climate warming, air and water quality, and energy consumption. Companies that show a concern for quality of life tend to enjoy a greater reputation, all other things being equal. These companies treat employees better and enjoy good relations with their suppliers and distributors.

We would like to suggest a seventh factor to add to Harris's list: *Innovation*. Innovation is both a process and a mindset within organizations that generates, implements, and diffuses ideas and new offerings that drive long-term growth. Without continuous innovation, organizations and their strategies will atrophy. And so will their reputations.

Companies that want to take a long-term view and prosper for a long period must address a series of five critical questions that go directly to the heart of the company's Business Enterprise Sustainability:

- What role does the company's reputation play among its stakeholders in helping to increase its chances of long-term prosperity? What actions can a company take to improve its reputation? (Company reputation)

- What steps can a company take to improve customer enthusiasm for its offerings in the hope of turning its customers into advocates who help market the company to others? (Customer advocacy)

- What factors seem to be most associated with company longevity? (Company longevity)

- Does the active practice of corporate social responsibility (CSR) and ecological sustainability (ES) add years to company longevity? (CSR and ES)

▪ Does the active practice of ethical and authentic behavior add years to company longevity? (Company ethics and authenticity)

The central point is that reputations are built over time. When they are strong, they will carry a company through crises and into a longer-lasting future. Such companies must maintain or enhance these seven factors during difficult periods of turbulence. Reputations can easily be damaged and in much less time than it took to build them. They can be lost overnight by a misjudgment, a scandal, or a slip in quality or integrity. A company that wants to live for a long time must manage these factors—and manage them carefully and diligently—in good times and especially in bad times.

CUSTOMER ENTHUSIASM AND ADVOCACY

Most companies strive to build a strong and satisfied base of customers who come back again and again to buy from the same company. It is easier to sell more to the same customers than to have to search for new customers. The aim is to build loyal customers and hope they will not only buy repeatedly from your company but tell others good things about your company as well. These loyal "customer advocates" or "customer evangelists" can be very important in the success of a company.

Fred Reichheld, an expert on customer loyalty, developed the Net Promoters Score (NPS), an instrument to measure customer advocacy, which he describes in his book, *The Ultimate Question.*[8] Reichheld shows how to turn customers into advocates and promoters. The key: one simple question that tracks promoters and detractors and produces a clear, easy-to-understand measure: *Would you feel comfortable recommending us to others?*

Now, if a customer answers, "I love your company and I have already been recommending it to others," that's a 10 on a 10-point scale. "I love your company, and although I haven't recommended it, I would feel completely comfortable doing that" scores a 9. "I love your company and if it comes up naturally in conversation, I would say good things about it" is an 8. And, of course, if a customer says, "I hate your company and I have already broadcast how bad you are," that would be the lowest score of 1.

To find the Net Promoters Score, subtract the percentage of customers who gave your company a score of 1 through 6 from the percentage of customers who scored your company an 8 through 10. According to Reichheld, companies with a high NPS also show higher long-term profitability.

The essence of the concept for creating loyalty is, as Reichheld asserts, to "show your partners [stakeholders such as customers and employees] that loyalty is a logical strategy for the pursuit of self-interest when self-interest is defined in the context of lifelong success."

Reichheld's six principles for building loyalty can be summed up as follows:[9]

1. Always play to provide wins for the stakeholders as well as for the company.

2. Be selective about the employees and customers a company takes on and encourages to stay with the company so that they enhance its cooperative system.

3. Adhere to the company's approach to being loyal (and earning loyalty in return). For example, "Do right by the customer" was an actionable motto for the software company Intuit when bugs cropped up in its tax software.

4. Reward the right results.

5. Listen, learn, act, and explain (communication is a dialogue, not a monologue).

6. Begin with how the company wants to be remembered, when deciding what to say and do today, and then preach with words and actions to support that end.

Some of Reichheld's high NPS achievers from the U.S. include Enterprise Rent-A-Car, Harley-Davidson, Cisco Systems, Dell Computers, the *New York Times,* and small business and consumer accounting and tax preparation software maker Intuit.

Reichheld also references companies such as Southwest Airlines in the U.S., as well as Germany's software leader SAP.

We need loyalty more than ever as the Internet allows us to become more and more distanced from the people with whom we work. Instead of spurning the Internet and its cold-hearted, digital ways, Reichheld embraces the electronic marketplace and sees it as a way for companies to deepen relationships with customers, employees, suppliers, and investors. He writes that he has found that trust actually rules the Web. More trust strengthens loyalty. When your online customers trust your website, they will share more of their personal information with you, which enables you to form more intimate customer relationships, which in turn allows you to serve your customers better with more personalized products and services. Reichheld writes that this kind of personal attention creates a virtuous cycle in which even more loyalty is created.[10]

If Reichheld is correct, the key question is how to build enthusiastic customers. In marketing terms, we say that the company must do better than just satisfying the customers: It needs to *delight* the customers. Some companies succeed in doing this—and doing it well—year after year.

The evidence is found in a new study published in a book called *Firms of Endearment.*[11] The three authors decided to ask a large sample of Americans to name one or more companies that they "loved" or would "dearly miss if these companies went bankrupt or disappeared."

Here are the companies that received such strong mentions by a large number of randomly chosen consumers in the U.S.: Amazon.com, BMW, Caterpillar, eBay, Google, Harley-Davidson, Honda, IKEA, Johnson & Johnson, New Balance, Patagonia, Southwest Airlines, Starbucks, Timberland, Toyota, and UPS.

The next question: Is there a recipe for becoming an *endeared company?* Are there any common characteristics that all these companies share? The answer is yes, according to the authors:

Common Characteristics of Firms of Endearment

- They align the interests of all stakeholder groups.

- Their executive salaries are relatively modest.

- They operate an open-door policy that allows access to top management.

- Their employee compensation and benefits are high for the category; their employee training is longer; and their employee turnover is lower.

- They hire people who are passionate about customers.

- They view suppliers as true partners who collaborate in improving productivity and quality and lowering costs.

- They believe that their corporate culture is their greatest asset and primary source of competitive advantage.

- Their marketing costs are much lower than their peers while customer satisfaction and retention is much higher.

CHARACTERISTICS OF COMPANIES THAT HAVE LIVED A LONG LIFE

Other observers have researched the characteristics of long-living organizations.

Arie de Geus spent thirty-eight years on three continents as a line manager at Royal Dutch Shell, finishing his career as the corporate planning director in charge of business and scenario planning. While at Shell, de Geus initiated a study of companies that have enjoyed long lives. He wanted to see if these companies were managed with a common set of traits and priorities. The more he examined companies, the more he became concerned about their life expectancy. He wrote, "The natural average lifespan of a corporation should be as long as two or three centuries."

De Geus quoted a Dutch survey of corporate life expectancy in Japan and Europe that came up with 12.5 years as the average life expectancy of a company. "The average life expectancy of a multinational corporation—Fortune 500 or its equivalent—is between 40 and 50 years," he wrote, further noting that a third of 1970s Fortune 500 companies had disappeared by 1993—acquired, merged, or broken to pieces. There are a few exceptions, such as Stora, which began more than 700 years ago as a copper mine in central Sweden, or Sumitomo, which had its origins in a copper-casting shop in Kyoto, Japan, founded in 1590. But de Geus says the wide gap between most companies' maximum possible life span and the average realization thereof represents huge wasted potential—and devastated work lives and communities.[12]

However, de Geus did find that in addition to some companies that are more than 500 years old, a number have lasted over 200 years, such as DuPont, which was founded in 1802. In all, he found thirty companies that have been around for at least 100 years. They include W. R. Grace (founded 1854), Kodak (founded 1888), Mitsui (founded 1876), and Siemens (founded 1847). He published his findings in the book *The Living Company*. His contention is simple:

that companies are living entities that can survive and thrive for centuries, provided they focus on selected aspects of their character and operations. His analysis revealed that companies that rose to the status of a "living company" had four distinct traits:[13]

- *Sensitivity to the world around them.* Long-lived companies sample, learn, and adapt to what is going on around them.

- *Awareness of their identity.* They are cohesive and have a strong sense of identity based on the ability to build a shared community.

- *Tolerance to new ideas.* They are patient, generally decentralized, with widespread decision-making authority, and tolerant of "noncore" activities on their periphery (which may well become tomorrow's core).

- *Conservatism in financing.* They are conservative with their money, which they use to govern their own growth and to give them options.

De Geus also found that the thirty long-lived companies he identified gave high priority to the following practices:

- Valuing people, not assets

- Loosening steering and control

- Organizing for learning

- Shaping the human community

In times of turbulence, companies are stressed, compressed, and tested at many levels, sometimes so much so that they cannot fully recover. While we have now entered The Age of Turbulence, it certainly doesn't mean that companies did not have to withstand great turbulence in the past—it was just more episodic and coincident with great disruptive events, such as cataclysmic depressions, wars, and other critical events in history. De Geus's list of living companies, all 100 or more years old, had lived through some of the most violent turbulence imaginable. Their ability to survive and to emerge even stronger was certainly helped by the traits and priorities identified by de Geus.

CORPORATE SOCIAL RESPONSIBILITY (CSR) AND ECOLOGICAL SUSTAINABILITY (ES)

Do companies that practice CSR and ES tend to live a longer life? We have noted the increasing interest of companies to show that they are humane and that they care for the environment and social problems. For example, American Express, Avon, Ben & Jerry's, and The Body Shop, have made significant commitments to social programs. These companies believe that they are making a difference, that their contributions are appreciated, and that they supply some basis for consumer preference if other things are equal among the competitors. Others have championed social causes that bound them even closer to the marketplace. Among companies that have demonstrated their commitment to social responsibility and the social causes they have championed are:[14]

Company	Social Cause
Aleve	*Arthritis*
Avon	*Breast cancer*
Best Buy	*Recycling used electronics*
British Airways	*Children in need*
General Mills	*Better nutrition*
General Motors	*Traffic safety*
Home Depot	*Habitat for Humanity*

Kraft Foods	*Reducing obesity*
Levi Strauss	*Preventing AIDS*
Motorola	*Reducing solid waste*
Pepsi-Cola	*Staying active*
Shell	*Coastal clean-up*
Starbucks	*Protecting tropical rainforests*

But in The Age of Turbulence, and especially in a period of financial meltdown, companies are likely to reconsider these commitments or scale down their funding. Here is where these companies have to proceed thoughtfully. They have achieved a certain positive image for caring. Abandoning these commitments wholesale could alter the attitudes of customers and other stakeholders. They would be abandoning worthwhile charitable organizations at a time when these organizations need the money the most. If reported in the press, this news could create negative feelings. Certainly if a company has a valid reason for terminating its support—having found that the money was not wisely spent or that the charity had troubled leadership, for example—it can in good conscience cut the funding. But if the company still feels that its funding to some organization is leading to good consequences, it may want to scale down some of the funding but not withdraw all support.

ETHICAL AND AUTHENTIC BEHAVIOR

Over time, companies acquire different reputations for ethical and authentic behavior. Most observers would say that General Electric, IBM, and Procter & Gamble have built ethical behavior into the soul of their companies. They depend not only on training and internalization, but also on publishing a clear set of guidelines and rules. One can also say that these companies have "authenticity."

They know their identities; they are transparent in their activities. They want to contrast themselves with fly-by-night shops, greed-driven financial manipulators, and those stealing money or cheating their stakeholders.

During periods of turbulence, the temptation is to cut down on promises and payment schedules and do anything to "save the ship." The former head of purchasing at General Motors, José Ignacio López de Arriortúa, was later accused of misappropriating trade secrets when he left the company in 1992 to join Volkswagen.[15] López, nicknamed "Super López" for his prowess in cutting costs at General Motors, would call a parts supplier in the evening and say, "We are paying you too much. We want to lower the contracted price by 15 percent. I will call you back in an hour to get your agreement." The parts supplier, who was in shock, had little recourse but to say yes. But this treatment created ill will among GM's parts suppliers. Subsequently, they became more cautious in their dealings with GM and would give preference to Ford and Chrysler when they had to allocate a shortage of parts to the Big Three. "Scalping" the suppliers or customers to gain a temporary advantage almost always boomerangs and hurts the short-term driven company.

So a company's internal and external behavior leaves a legacy that affects the stakeholders' future mindsets and behavior toward the company. Oftentimes this reveals the absence of the company's authenticity, a quality that is becoming increasingly important to consumers.

In their book *Authenticity: What Consumers Really Want,* James Gilmore and Joseph Pine describe this growing trend, "In our increasingly experience-driven world, consumers crave what's authentic. It's a paradox of today's Experience Economy: The more contrived the world seems, the more we all demand what's real. As reality is qualified, altered, and commercialized, consumers respond to what is engaging, personal, memorable—and above all, authentic. If customers don't view your offerings as real, you'll be branded inauthentic—fake!—and risk losing credibility, customers, and ultimately the sale." [16]

But what's authentic? Gilmore and Pine define what authenticity means to the postmodern consumer, and how companies can render their offerings as "really real."

Because of the shift to what Gilmore and Pine termed the "experience economy," products and services are no longer enough for companies to create and sell; today's consumers and businesses want *experiences*—memorable events that personally engage them. And in a world increasingly filled with deliberately, sensationally staged events and impersonal transactions, consumers and businesses base whether to buy on how real they perceive an offering. Business today, especially as everyone and every company is being racked by turbulence, is increasingly becoming all about being real, original, genuine, sincere, and authentic.

Conclusion

As we began our exploration of turbulence and chaos, it was our stated hope that *Chaotics* would help business leaders to develop a keener sense of the new challenges that await them and their companies as they begin to realize and take stock of the *new normality*—heightened turbulence and chaos.

To cope with the new environment, in Chapter 1 we identified the many factors creating turbulence that require business leaders to adopt new strategic behaviors if they are to reduce their vulnerabilities and increase their opportunities quickly and systematically.

In Chapter 2 we described the normal cut-and-run responses of business executives to periods of recession and turbulence, and how these responses often damage the company's long-term viability. They need a more thoughtful response based not only on correcting weaknesses but on spotting and seizing new opportunities.

In Chapter 3, we showed how many smart and experienced executives continue to be surprised by the events unfolding around them, even though many of these events are visible to the trained eye. By providing guidance in the development of an effective early warning system to detect turbulence in the environment, and constructing yet-foreseen scenarios and strategies, we offered a way to build new and robust organizational muscle to handle the turbulence, including heightened turbulence, with decisiveness and speed.

In Chapter 4, we described new behaviors that are required—behaviors that are *responsive, robust,* and *resilient.* We discussed how each management function in the organization needs to distinguish between what it can cut or delay, what it can outsource, and what it can increase or accelerate to improve its short-term and long-term performance.

Chapter 5 outlined how companies can sharpen their marketing and sales tools as well as their strategies in turbulent times when there's pressure to cut budgets in these areas. In turbulent times, and most definitely heightened turbulent times, one can argue that the company needs to increase its marketing muscle, not reduce it, if it is to lay the groundwork for a stronger and longer future.

And finally in Chapter 6, we showed how companies must balance short- and long-term considerations in developing their strategies; how they must maintain and enhance the major factors affecting their reputations; how they can create a company to which people feel loyal and would sorely miss if it disappeared; and how creating customer advocates is a sure way to generate positive word-of-mouth that will attract and win new customers.

If we have achieved our stated goal, *Chaotics* now provides business leaders with the system and tools to successfully navigate through the uncertain waters that will continue to confront all of their businesses in this new era, The Age of Turbulence.

N O T E S

INTRODUCTION

1. Peter Drucker, *The Age of Discontinuity* (New York: HarperCollins Publications, 1992).

2. Andy Grove, *Only the Paranoid Survive* (New York: Current Doubleday Random House Publishers, 1999).

3. Alan Greenspan, *The Age of Turbulence: Adventures in a New World* (New York: Penguin, 2007).

4. Clayton Christensen, *Business Innovation and Disruptive Technology: Harnessing the Power of Breakthrough Technology for Competitive Advantage* (Upper Saddle River, NJ: Financial Times Prentice Hall Books, 2003).

CHAPTER 1

1. National Intelligence Council, *Global Trends 2025: A Transformed World* (Washington, DC: U.S. Government Printing Office, November 2008); www.dni.gov/.

2. "India under attack," *The Economist,* November 27, 2008; http://www.economist.com/.

3. Andrew S. Grove, *Only the Paranoid* Survive (New York: Currency Doubleday Random House Publishers, 1999).

4. Tom Mullin, "Turbulent times for fluids," *New Scientist,* November 11, 1989, http://www.fortunecity.com/.

5. "Chaos theory," http://en.wikipedia.org/.

6. "Butterfly effect," Wikipedia, http://en.wikipedia.org/.

7. "Business turbulence," BNET Business Dictionary, http://dictionary.bnet.com/.

8. Patrick M. Fitzgibbons, "Bernanke offers bleak outlook," September 24, 2008, Reuters, http://uk.reuters.com/.

9. "Financial crisis needs unprecedented responses," *GEO World*, http://www.geo.tv/.

10. "Stock market suffers largest drop ever, experts say," *GreenvilleOnline.com*, September 29, 2008, http://www.greenvilleonline.com/; Tim Paradis, "Dow Climbs More Than 900 Points," KUTV Online, October 13, 2008, http://www.kutv.com/; "Whiplash Ends a Roller Coaster Week," *New York Times*, October, 10, 2008, http://www.nytimes.com/.

11. "Fear grips global stock markets," BBC, October 10, 2008, http://news.bbc.co.uk/.

12. "Worst financial crisis in human history: Bank boss's warning as pound suffers biggest fall for 37 years," *Daily Mail*, October 25, 2008, http://www.dailymail.co.uk/.

13. "Fear grips global stock markets," BBC.

14. Dan Wilchins and Jonathan Stempel, "U.S. rescues Citi with $20 billion capital," Reuters, November 24, 2008, http://www.reuters.com/.

15. "Information Technology and Globalization," *Global Envision*, February 15, 2006; http://www.globalenvision.org/.

16. "Cloud computing," Wikipedia, http://en.wikipedia.org/.

17. "Let it rise," *The Economist*, October 23, 2008, http://www.economist.com/specialreports/displayStory.cfm?story_id=12411882; and "The long nimbus," *The Economist*, October 23, 2008, http://www.economist.com/.

18. "The long nimbus," *The Economist*.

19. "Computers without borders," *The Economist*, October 23, 2008, http://www.economist.com/.

20. "Microsoft Sharepoint," Wikipedia, http://en.wikipedia.org/.

21. *The Innovator's Dilemma: When New Technologies Cause Great Firms to Fail*, by Clayton M. Christensen, Harvard Business School Press, Cambridge, MA, 1997.

22. *The Innovator's Solution: Creating and Sustaining Successful Growth*, by Clayton M. Christensen and Michael E. Raynor, Harvard Business School Press, Cambridge, MA, 1997.

23. Joseph Schumpeter, *Capitalism, Socialism, and Democracy*, 3rd ed. (1942; repr., New York: Harper & Row, 1950).

24. "Disruptive technology," Wikipedia, http://en.wikipedia.org/.

25. Ibid.

26. "The blood of incumbents," *The Economist,* October 28, 2004, http://www.economist.com/.

27. Harold L. Vogel, "Disruptive Technologies and Disruptive Thinking," *Michigan State Law Review* 2005, no. 1, https://www.msu.edu/.

28. "The blood of incumbents," *The Economist.*

29. Fareed Zakaria, "The Rise of the Rest," *Newsweek,* May 12, 2008, http://www.newsweek.com/.

30. Ibid.

31. "China resists contribution to IMF bailout fund," *China Economic Review,* November 17, 2008, http://www.chinaeconomicreview.com/.

32. "The credit crunch: China moves to centre stage," *The Economist,* October 30, 2008, http://www.economist.com/.

33. Reuters, "*Fortune* 500 list: US companies' worst show in 10 years," *The Economic Times,* July 10, 2008, http://economictimes.indiatimes.com/.

34. Harold L. Sirkin, James W. Hemerling, and Arindam K. Bhattacharya, *Globality: Competing with Everyone from Everywhere for Everything* (New York: Business Plus, 2008), http://www.washingtonpost.com/.

35. "A bigger world," *The Economist,* September 18, 2008, http://www.economist.com/.

36. "Hypercompetition," Wikipedia, http://en.wikipedia.org/.

37. Richard D'Aveni, *Hypercompetition: Managing the Dynamics of Strategic Maneuvering* (New York: Free Press, 2004).

38. Ibid.

39. Ibid.

40. Ibid.

41. "Sovereign wealth fund," Wikipedia, http://en.wikipedia.org/.

42. "A bigger world," *The Economist.*

43. "The End of Arrogance: America Loses Its Dominant Economic Role": Spiegel Online, September 30, 2008, http://www.spiegel.de/international/world/.

44. Alia McMullen. "U.S. faces longest recession in 20 years," *Financial Post,* October 21, 2008, http://www.financialpost.com.

45. "Sovereign Funds Become Big Speculators," *Washington Post,* August 12, 2008, http://www.washingtonpost.com/.

46. Reuters, "Sarkozy wants Europe sovereign fund to fight crisis," October 21, 2008, http://www.reuters.com/.

47. "A bigger world," *The Economist.*

48. "From risk to opportunity—How global executives view sociopolitical issues: McKinsey Global Survey Results," *McKinsey Quarterly,* October 2008.

49. Marcel W. Brinkman, Nick Hoffman, and Jeremy M. Oppenheim, "How climate change could affect corporate valuations," *McKinsey Quarterly,* October 2008, http://www.mckinseyquarterly.com/.

50. Anna Kirah, "Concept making," http://www.kirahconsult.com/.

51. "Losing face: A tale of two airlines and their Facebook fiascos," *The Economist,* November 6, 2008, http://www.economist.com/.

52. Reuters, "Global Study Reveals Customer Empowerment as Chief Driver of Online Business Through 2013," June 2008, http://www.reuters.com/.

53. Peter F. Drucker, *Managing in Turbulent Times* (New York: Harper-Collins, 1980).

CHAPTER 2
1. Warren E. Buffett, "Buy American. I Am," *New York Times,* October 16, 2008, Op-Ed section, http://www.nytimes.com/.

2. Caroline Brothers, "Budget airlines' strategy is split," *International Herald Tribune,* November 18, 2008, http://www.iht.com/.

3. Ibid.

4. Christian Wienberg and Tasneem Brogger, "Sterling Airlines of Denmark Is Declared Bankrupt," Bloomberg, October 29, 2008, http://www.bloomberg.com/.

5. Richard F. Dobbs, Tomas Karakolev, and Francis Malige, "Learning to Love Recessions," *McKinsey Quarterly,* June 2002, http://www.mckinseyquarterly.com/.

6. Information and comments on Goldman Sachs come from several sources: "Record Earnings Seen for Goldman Sachs, Based on Hedge Funds," *International Herald Tribune,* October 8, 2007; "Goldman Sachs Escaped Subprime Collapse by Selling Subprime Bonds Short," *Daily*

Reckoning, October 19, 2007; "Southern National Bancorp Reports 3rd Quarter After-Tax Profit of $588 Thousand, an Increase of 26 Percent over the Same Quarter of 2007, Before Loss on Freddie Mac Perpetual Preferred Stock of $1.3 Million," *iStockAnalyst,* October 27, 2008, http://www.istockanalyst.com/; "AIG's Fed Bailout Reaches $143.8 Billion," *TheStreet.com,* October 31, 2008, http://www.thestreet.com/; and Frank H. Knight, *Risk, Uncertainty, and Profit* (Boston, MA: Hart, Schaffner & Marx; Houghton Mifflin, 1921), as referenced in "Frank Knight," Wikipedia, http://en.wikipedia.org/.

7. Rita McGrath, "Cut Costs like Avon—Not Home Depot," *Harvard Business Online,* August 29, 2008; available at http://www.businessweek.com/.

8. Joseph A. Avila, Nathaniel J. Mass, and Mark P. Turchan, "Is Your Growth Strategy Your Worst Enemy?" *McKinsey Quarterly,* May 1995, http://www.mckinseyquarterly.com/.

9. Diamond Management & Technology Consultants, "Focus, Not Across-the-Board Budget Cuts, the Key to Success During a Recession," news release, October 13, 2008; available at http://ca.news.finance.yahoo.com/.

10. Ibid.

11. "Opportunities—and Obstacles—for the B2B Market in Tough Economic Times," *Knowledge@Wharton,* October 29, 2008, http://knowledge.wharton.upenn.edu/.

12. "10 Worst Innovation Mistakes in a Recession," *BusinessWeek,* January 13, 2008, http://www.businessweek.com/.

13. Ian Davis, "Learning to Grow Again," *McKinsey Quarterly,* February 2004, http://www.mckinseyquarterly.com/.

14. Our list of the three biggest marketing mistakes to avoid is derived from Steve McKee, "Five Don'ts for Marketing in Tough Times," *BusinessWeek,* July 11, 2008, http://www.businessweek.com/.

15. "10 Worst Innovation Mistakes in a Recession," *BusinessWeek.*

16. Diamond Management & Technology Consultants, "Focus, Not Across-the-Board Budget Cuts, the Key to Success During a Recession."

17. "New menu items, $1 menu, game boost McDonald's sales," *Chicago Tribune,* November 10, 2008, http://www.chicagotribune.com/.

18. "Coffee wars," *The Economist,* January 10, 2008, http://www.economist.com/.

19. "Starbucks profit falls 97 percent on fewer customers and rising costs," *LA Times,* November 11, 2008, http://www.latimes.com/.

20. Bill Tancer, "Brewing Battle: Starbucks vs. McDonald's," *Time,* January 10, 2008, http://www.time.com/.

21. Brad Sugars, "7 Biggest Mistakes in Setting Prices," *Entrepreneur.com,* August 26, 2008, http://www.entrepreneur.com/.

22. "Transactional Customers vs. Relational Customers," Adcouver Blog, posting from February 20, 2006, http://ashtonmedia.blogspot.com/.

23. Diamond Management & Technology Consultants, "Focus, Not Across-the-Board Budget Cuts, the Key to Success During a Recession."

24. Richard Blandy et al., *Does Training Pay? Evidence from Australian Enterprises* (Adelaide: National Centre for Vocational Education Research, 2002), http://www.ncver.edu.au/.

25. Stephen Kozicki, *The Creative Negotiator* (Sydney: Bennelong Publishing, 2005).

26. Jane C. Linder and Brian McCarthy, "When Good Management Shows, Creating Value in an Uncertain Economy" (research report, Accenture Institute for Strategic Change, Cambridge, MA, September 2002), http://www.accenture.com/.

27. "Heads will roll at Citi," *Economist.com,* November 17, 2008, http://www.economist.com/; "Citigroup Troubles Grow," *U.S. News & World Report,* November 14, 2008, http://www.usnews.com/; and Reuters, "Citigroup gets massive government bailout," November 24, 2008, http://www.reuters.com/.

CHAPTER 3
1. Lord John Browne, "Lord Goold Memorial Lecture: Marketing Strategy" (speech, Bradford University, London, November 23, 2001), http://www.bp.com/.

2. Michael Lewis, "The End," *Portfolio.com,* December 2008, http://www.portfolio.com/.

3. Lowell Bryan and Diana Farrell, "Leading through uncertainty," *McKinsey Quarterly,* December 2008, http://www.mckinseyquarterly.com/.

4. Andrew S. Grove, *Only the Paranoid Survive* (New York: Currency Doubleday Random House Publishers, 1999).

5. "As Goldman and Morgan Shift, a Wall St. Era Ends," *New York Times*, September 21, 2008, http://dealbook.blogs.nytimes.com/.

6. Gary Hamel and Liisa Välikangas, "The Quest for Resilience," *Harvard Business Review*, September 2003.

7. George S. Day and Paul J. H. Schoemaker, *Peripheral Vision: Detecting the Weak Signals That Will Make or Break Your Company* (Cambridge, MA: Harvard Business School Press, 2006).

8. George S. Day and Paul J. H. Schoemaker, "Scanning the Periphery," *Harvard Business Review*, November 2005.

9. Ibid.

10. Ibid.

11. Benjamin Gilad, *Early Warning: Using Competitive Intelligence to Anticipate Market Shifts, Control Risk, and Create Powerful Strategies* (New York: AMACOM, 2003).

12. "Honda opens new plant while Big Three wither," *Domain-B.Com*, November 20, 2008, http://www.domain-b.com/.

13. Peter Schwartz, *Inevitable Surprises: Thinking Ahead in a Time of Turbulence* (New York: Gotham Books, 2004).

14. "Scenario Planning," Wikipedia, http://en.wikipedia.org/.

15. Hugh G. Courtney, Jane Kirkland, and S. Patrick Viguerie, "Strategy under uncertainty," *McKinsey Quarterly*, June 2000, http://www.mckinsey quarterly.com/.

16. David J. Snowden and Mary E. Boone, "A Leader's Framework for Decision Making," *Harvard Business Review*, November 2007.

17. Ibid.

18. This method is described in "Scenario Planning," Wikipedia.

19. Ibid.

20. Paul Krugman, "Lest We Forget," *The New York Times*, November 27, 2008, http://www.nytimes.com/.

21. Southwest Airlines, "Southwest Airlines Reports Fourth Quarter Earnings and 35th Consecutive Year of Profitability," news release, January 23, 2008, http://www.southwest.com/.

22. Kevin Buehler, Andrew Freeman, and Ron Hulme, "The Risk Revolution | The Strategy: Owning the Right Risks," *Harvard Business Review*, September 2008.

CHAPTER 4

1. G. K. Chesterton, *The Scandal of Father Brown* (New York: Dodd, Mead & Company, 1935).

2. "2008 U.S. Bank Failures Now Stands at 22," Clips & Comment blog, November 25, 2008, http://www.clipsandcomment.com/.

3. "Responsiveness," Wikipedia, http://en.wikipedia.org/; "Robustness," Wikipedia, http://en.wikipedia.org/; "Resilience," Wikipedia, http://en.wikipedia.org/.

4. Hermann Simon, *Hidden Champions: Lessons from 500 of the World's Best Unknown Companies* (Cambridge, MA: Harvard Business School Press, 1996).

5. Hermann Simon, *Hidden Champions of the Twenty-First Century* (New York: Springer Publishing Company, 2009).

6. Wesley R. Elsberry, "Punctuated Equilibria," The TalkOrigins Archive, http://www.talkorigins.org/.

7. Simon, *Hidden Champions of the Twenty-First Century.*

8. Lucy Kellaway, "The year of the CFO," *The Economist,* November 19, 2008, http://www.economist.com/.

9. "Take a deep breath," *The Economist,* January 19, 2006, http://www.economist.com/.

10. Ibid.

11. Richard Dobbs, Tomas Karakolev, and Rishi Raj, "Preparing for the next downturn," *McKinsey Quarterly,* April 2007, http://www.mckinsey quarterly.com/.

12. Ibid.

13. Ibid.

14. Ibid.

15. Brian Murray and the Gartner client quoted in Alan Cane, "How to survive an IT squeeze," *Financial Times,* November 4, 2008, http://www.ft.com/.

16. James M. Kaplan, Roger P. Roberts, and Johnson Sikes, "Managing IT in a downturn: Beyond cost cutting," *McKinsey Quarterly,* September 2008, http://www.mckinseyquarterly.com/.

17. Hugh Pinkus, "Surviving a Recession: Keeping Manufacturing Profits Up When the Economy Is Down," *IndustryWeek,* October 24, 2008, http://www.industryweek.com/.

18. Ibid.

19. "Partners in wealth," *The Economist,* January 19, 2006: http://www.economist.com/.

20. Ibid.

21. Pinkus, "Surviving a Recession: Keeping Manufacturing Profits Up When the Economy Is Down," *IndustryWeek.*

22. Fayazuddin A Shirazi, "10 Actions to Ride Out a Recession," *Chief Executive,* July/August 2008, http://www.chiefexecutive.net/.

23. Chip W. Hardt, Nicolas Reinecke, and Peter Spiller, "Inventing the 21st-century purchasing organization," *McKinsey Quarterly,* November 2007, http://www.mckinseyquarterly.com/.

24. Brian R. Robinson, "Purchasing Best Practices: Ten Keys to Effective Purchasing," Institute of Management Consultants, March 20, 2006, http://www.imcstlouis.org/.

25. Lindsay Blakely, "How to Manage Your Team in a Downturn (and Come Out on Top)," *BNET.com,* June 23, 2008, http://www.bnet.com/.

CHAPTER 5
1. Fred Geyer and Chiaki Nishino, "Making Marketing Smarter Amidst the Cuts," *Prophet Newsletter,* December 2008, http://www.prophet.com/.

CHAPTER 6
1. Carl von Clausewitz, *On War,* trans. Michael Howard and Peter Paret, (Princeton, NJ: Princeton University Press, 1976; rev. ed. 1984), based on the original in German, *Vom Kriege* (Berlin: Dummlers Verlag, 1832).

2. Lenny T. Mendonca and Jeremy Oppenheim, "Investing in sustainability: An interview with Al Gore and David Blood," *McKinsey Quarterly,* May 2007, http://www.mckinseyquarterly.com/.

3. "The Essential Tension: How to Reconcile New vs. Old to Achieve Breakthrough Innovation in a Large Organization," presentation by Vijay Govinkarajan at *Leaders in London,* London, UK. December 4, 2008.

4. Ibid.

5. Roland Jones, "Chinese automakers are looking west," MSNBC.com, April 26, 2007, http://www.msnbc.msn.com/.

6. Harris Interactive, "Seventy-One Percent of Consumers Say the Reputation of Corporate America Is 'Poor,' but Consumers Will Buy, Recommend, and Invest in Companies that Concentrate on Building Their Corporate Reputation," news release, June 23, 2008, http://www.harrisinteractive.com/.

7. "100 Best Companies to Work For, 2008," *Fortune,* http://money.cnn.com/.

8. Fred Reichheld, *The Ultimate Question* (Cambridge, MA: Harvard Business School Press, 2001).

9. Ibid.

10. Chris Lauer, "Loyalty Rules!: How Today's Leaders Build Lasting Relationships," review of *Loyalty Rules!* by Frederick F. Reichheld, *BusinessWeek,* June 10, 2008, http://www.businessweek.com/.

11. Rajendra S. Sisodia, David B. Wolfe, and Jagdish N. Sheth, *Firms of Endearment* (Upper Saddle River, NJ: Wharton School Publishing, 2007).

12. Julia Flynn, "The Biology of Business," review of *The Living Company: Habits for Survival in a Turbulent Business Environment,* by Arie de Geus, *BusinessWeek,* July 4, 1997, http://www.businessweek.com/.

13. Arie de Geus, *The Living Company* (MA: Longview Publishing Limited, 2002).

14. Philip Kotler and Nancy R. Lee, *Corporate Social Responsibility: Doing the Most Good for Your Company and Your Cause* (New York: John Wiley, 2005).

15. Emma Daly, "Spain Court Refuses to Extradite Man G.M. Says Took Its Secrets," *New York Times,* June 20, 2001, http://query.nytimes.com/.

16. James H. Gilmore and B. Joseph Pine II, *Authenticity: What Consumers Really Want* (Cambridge, MA: Harvard Business School Publishing, 2007).

INDEX

ABOUT THE AUTHORS

Philip Kotler, considered by many to be the father of modern marketing, is the S. C. Johnson & Son Distinguished Professor of International Marketing at the Kellogg School of Management, Northwestern University. He received his Master's degree at the University of Chicago and his Ph.D. degree at MIT, both in economics. He did post-doctoral work in mathematics at Harvard University and in behavioral science at the University of Chicago. He published his 13th edition of *Marketing Management,* the world's leading textbook in teaching marketing to MBAs. He has also published *Marketing Models, Principles of Marketing, Strategic Marketing for Nonprofit Organizations, Social Marketing, Marketing Places, Corporate Social Responsibility,* and 30 other books. His research covers strategic marketing, innovation, consumer marketing, business marketing, services marketing, distribution, e-marketing, and social marketing. He has been a consultant to IBM, Bank of America, Merck, Ford, General Electric, Honeywell, and many other companies. He has received 12 honorary doctorate degrees from major universities in the U.S. and abroad.

John A. Caslione is a recognized expert on the global economy who has executed business strategies in 88 countries on 6 continents. He serves as adviser to large and middle market companies, including ABB, Becton-Dickenson Biosciences, Caltex Lubricants,

ExxonMobil, GE, Hewlett-Packard, Johnson & Johnson, IBM, and Philips N.V. He is founder and president of global mergers and acquisitions adviser GCS Business Capital LLC, and was also founder and president of Andrew-Ward International, Inc., an international management consultancy. He speaks at numerous conferences globally, including as guest lecturer at Northwestern University's Kellogg School of Management, where he speaks on the global economy, global marketing, and global business development, including emerging markets. He has authored four books on globalization and developing global business strategies, including in emerging markets. He received his MBA from the University of New York (Buffalo) and his Juris Doctor from Chicago-Kent College of Law (Chicago). He is a founding member of Rotary International's first English-speaking member club in Frankfurt, Germany, in 2006.